RAGE !

How An Adoption Ignited a Fire

by
Lori Carangelo

Access Press

Cover photo: Richard Gregory Mox, age 21 in 1992

Printed in the United States of America
ISBN: 978-0-942605-47-1

CONTENTS

PART 1:
HOW GREGORY MOX'S ADOPTION IGNITED A FIRE - 5

PART 2:
HOW OTHER ADOPTIONS IGNITED A FIRE - 67

PART 1:
HOW GREGORY MOX'S ADOPTION IGNITED A FIRE

"Curiosity is lying in wait for every secret."
-Ralph Waldo Emerson

Chapter 1.
WHY ?

Gregory Richard Mox was born August 16, 1970. In 1992, at age 21, that was still all he knew of his pre-adoption existence.

In the early hours on Friday, March 27, 1992, the quiet, neatly manicured, middle class suburb of Roseville, Michigan, was awakened by the screaming of a sirens, the bellow of a horn, flashing lights and the screech of tires at the brick bungalow in the 30700 block of Ferntree. Plumes of smoke rising from the home of Richard and Carol Mox obliterated the sunrise. A newspaper carrier had spotted the fire at 5:07 a.m. and called 911 a minute before a call from Joseph Booza was recorded. Awakened by smoke, the Mox's 21-year old son, Gregory, broke his bedroom window to escape the fire and ran across the street in his slipper, pajamas and robe to the Booza's house yelling

"My house is on fire and my parents are inside!"

Greg and Joe Booza went back to the Mox home but there was no response from inside when they called out and although Greg had the house keys in his pocket, they could not have reached the Moxes - their bedroom was already engulfed in flames. People on Ferntree who emerged from their homes in robes and slippers were just standing in the street watching and waiting when the firefighters, paramedics and police arrived. The month before, February 4th, there had been a fire at Margaret Guzik's home across the street from the Moxes and Guzik complained that at least 15 minutes had elapsed before fire fighters arrived but Roseville Fire Chief Morely Ireland had said that computer records showed crews arrived in 5 minutes. A fire engine arrived at the Mox house at 5:17 a.m. 10 minutes from the first 911 call, but it seems to take forever when you're watching something burn. Chief Morely thought about another house fire –

the one in December on Rudland Street in the same subdivision – a woman died in that fire.

Was there a serial arsonist in Roseville?

As the ceiling collapsed in an explosion of flames, everyone knew there was no hope of rescuing the Moxes.

Neighbors told reporters that, just prior to the couple's deaths, Richard Mox, 57, an assembly line worker at Ford Motor Company's Utica Trim plant since 1974, was practicing French for his upcoming performance in "Samson and Delilah," with the Michigan Open Theatre Choir.

Carol Mox, 54, a receptionist at a data processing firm in Troy for the past 6 years, had just won the chance to sing a solo with the Fraser Chorale and also been awarded a trip to Las Vegas for being an outstanding employee.

As for their adopted son, Greg, neighbors described him as "a quiet computer whiz." A former fellow employee at Greg's former job said "This guy is brilliant – He lived on his computer. He's a good person, very caring." Reverend Arthur Fauser of Our Lady Queen of All Saints Catholic Church would later tell a police investigator that the Mox family had attended church since 1964 and that Greg was such a gentle person.

But when the bodies of Richard and Carol Mox were pulled out of the still smoldering house that Friday, Assistant Prosecutor Steven Kaplan theorized that Greg and his parents were at odds over the lifestyle he had been living. Carol Mox's sister, Louise Iacobel, said Greg's parents routinely supported or "covered" for him, even when he got in trouble – that Greg was a substance abuser who stole from his adoptive parents and once broke into the Iacobel's Grosse Point Woods home – and that she thought Greg was "an angry young man." But no one seemed to have the answer as to **WHY** Greg would want to *murder* his adoptive parents.

The first known case of parricide in the United States was that of Lizzie Borden in 1886. Although acquitted, in the public's mind, she remains accused of the remorseless axe murder of her father and stepmother. Ever since, adoptees seem to be over-represented as "problem children" a well as parent killers.

Carol Anderson, MSW, JD, adoptee and former Director of a residential facility for troubled teenagers, reports that "about one-third of the teens admitted were adoptees, almost all of whom were adopted as infants" (CUB Newsletter of Concerned United Birthparents, March 1990). Since then, studies of adoptees who kill find no "bad seed" in common. And while some adopted killers were physically or sexually abused before or after being adopted, other adopted killers experienced no physical or sexual abuse. For lack of a reason in those cases, an easy conclusion is alleged that they were after the parents' estate, or that they are simply mentally ill. Yet for an adopted child and adult, what screws him up most in life is the picture in his head of "how it's *supposed* to be" and the blank page were his pre-adoption history should be.

Trials and news stories about adoptees who killed all seem to have a familiar ring – The adoptee showed **"no remorse"** for the killing, **no feelings** for their victims, and **no clear motive**. Rarely does the fact of the killer's adoptive status become a mitigating issue in his defense at trial.

Roseville Detective Lieutenant Joseph Steenland commented to the Macomb Daily, "It's a rough one to figure out. What can make you kill your parents?"

When an adoptee commits parricide, the "trigger" or proximate cause can be extremely subtle, because the root cause goes back to the moment that the child was transformed into an adoptee. And the connection between adoption and murder may be too subtle for a jury to grasp.

The only person who could really explain that connection in this case was Greg Mox, and I had no idea what to expect when I first wrote him. I was only sure of one thing – I wanted him to tell his story in his own words.

9

"Your children are a blessing;
Either that, or they want to kill you."
-Lanie Kazan, in "The Crew"

Chapter 2:
CORRESPONDENCE WITH A KILLER

On April 8, 1999, I wrote to Greg Mox who was then in prison and I explained:

> "A woman in Ann Arbor, Barbara Anderson-Kari, recalled reading about your case. She's a mother-turned-activist and suggested I might be interested in contacting you to exchange some information that might be useful to us both. I then found six news clippings from the Macomb Daily, 1992-1995, which gave me your defense lawyer's name, Edward Servitto. Only one of the six articles referred to your parents as *adoptive* parents confirming you are adopted. The woman who answered when I phoned Servitto said they had represented you but would not confirm that you are adopted nor discuss anything with me due to confidentiality. She suggested I contact you directly. The Michigan Department of Corrections, Lansing, gave me your location."

The preliminaries out of the way, I got to the point.

> According to the news clips, you were sentenced to life Without Parole on two counts of murdering your adoptive parents and one count for Arson.

Then I asked him point blank:

"Did you do it?"

Greg did not delay his reply, but his words seemed measured as if careful to sound self-assured and mature.

If handwriting in any way mirrors the soul, Greg's printing, rather than script handwriting, is distinctive from the thousands of adoptees' letters I've received over the years. His letters are drawn with deliberate geometric precision on invisible lines, probably by placing lined paper beneath. The letter 'y' always forms precisely the same 45-degree angle wherever it appears on the page, while all upper case letters, as well as lower case b, d, f, h, k, l, and t, have a deliberate backward curve. He similarly prints his signature, with a geometric logo after it. There is no break between his first and last name in his signature, as if to punctuate the uniqueness of his life with a unique hand.

He began:

> "Dear Lori, If I'd chosen a positive manner of expressing my extreme displeasure with the institution of adoption, I could presently be assisting you rather than accruing displeasure with the institution in which I dwell."

And then, dramatically placed on a line by itself, he added,

"Yes, I did it."

From the 1940s through the early 1960s, social work theory was predicated on the belief that secrecy as to the fact of the child's adoptive status was necessary to 'protect' the child from the stigma of 'illegitimacy.' In the 1960s to the 1970s when Greg was adopted, social workers began encouraging adoptive parents to tell the child of his adoptive status as soon as he is old enough to grasp the meaning of 'adopted.' But little or no true information about the child's pre-adoption past was shared, leaving adoptive parents without answers to their children's resulting questions.

Roseville couple die in early morning blaze

BY MARTY HAIR
Free Press Staff Writer

Richard Mox was practicing French for his upcoming performance in "Samson and Delilah" with the Michigan Opera Theatre choir.

Carol Mox had just won the chance to sing a solo with the Fraser Chorale and also had been awarded a trip to Las Vegas for being an outstanding employee.

Friends mourned Friday that the Roseville couple's rewards will never be realized. The Moxes — Richard, 57, and Carol, 54 — died in an early morning fire that swept the rear bedroom of their brick home in the 30700 block of Ferntree Street.

Police and fire officials said they didn't know what caused the fire.

Awakened by smoke, the couple's 21-year-old son Gregory, a Macomb Community College student, broke his bedroom window to escape and ran across the street to the home of Joseph Booza.

"He yelled, 'My house is on fire and my parents are inside!' " Booza said. They called 911 and went back to the Mox home but could not reach the couple, who were dead when fire fighters arrived. The cause of death was not immediately known.

A Free Press carrier who spotted the fire called 911 at 5:07 a.m., a minute before Booza's call was recorded.

A fire engine arrived at 5:17, followed almost immediately by other rescue vehicles, said Police Inspector Ron MacKool.

Neighbors said there had been concern about emergency response times after a Feb. 4 blaze at the home of Margaret Guzik, across the street from the Moxes. Guzik said at least 15 minutes elapsed before fire fighters arrived, but Roseville Fire Chief Morley Ireland said computer records show crews arrived in five minutes.

"When people are standing watching something burn and waiting for the fire department to arrive, it seems like it takes forever but it really doesn't," he said.

In December, a woman died in a house fire on Rudland Street in the same subdivision. Ireland said it was rare to have three fires in an area in four months, but there were no apparent links among them.

Richard Mox had been an assembly line worker at Ford Motor Co.'s Utica Trim plant since 1974. Carol Mox had been a receptionist at FIserv Galaxy Data Center in Troy, a data processing firm, for six years.

They moved to Ferntree Street about 26 years ago, Booza said, and raised their two daughters and son there.

Fraser Chorale director Patrick Pascaretti, who also directed them in the St. Joan of Arc church choir in St. Clair Shores, said they were talented musicians who loved to sing and dance, socialize and help others. Richard Mox had sung second tenor with Michigan Opera Theatre for more than a decade.

Carol Mox — called "Mother Mox" by coworkers for her caring ways — had won a solo in the Fraser Chorale's May program. She was to sing an old standard, "I Don't Know Why."

Funeral arrangements were being made by Wujek Calcaterra Funeral Home in Sterling Heights.

Detroit Free Press,
Saturday, March 28, 1992, Metro, p. 28

A Catholic Charities handbook titled *"Adoption Search: An Ethical Guide for Professionals"* prepared by Patricia Martinez Dorner, MA, LPC, LMFT (1977), used for educating social workers, contains the following:

> "There will be situations where it comes to light that untruths were told at the time of the adoption.
>
> Correcting these misrepresentations is necessary. There will be ramifications that call upon the professionalism and highest standards put forth by the agency. Unfortunately, there were those who were given incorrect information... When the practice of orientation changed and post-adoption services were extended, discovery about the un-truths traumatized and angered the deceived parents. There is no way to justify the deception. Perhaps one can look at the secretive nature of the closed adoption practice and frame it from that standpoint. Current professionals must seek ethical services while not assuming blame for the actions of their predecessors."

Greg continued,

> "My adoptive sister, Diane, first told me that I am half French-Canadian and half German. Later, she said I am actually Italian-Austrian and it was *she* who is French-German. I am far more Frankish in appearance than she. She has dark hair and eyes. I doubt she remembered correctly. Truly, I don't know, but I *am* curious."

I asked Greg how she had come up with that information, but Greg didn't know. He only knew that the Mox's adopted him and his two adoptive sisters from the same Catholic Services of Macomb, Michigan. I asked "Have you ever attempted to locate your family?"

> "I never made a concerted effort to find my family, partly because my adopters insisted it was nearly

impossible, but mostly due to my *pride*. I wished to have substantial success before meeting them. But, after killing their surrogates, I felt it would humiliate me further, alarm them, and burden them with guilt. By now, I'm less finicky and I certainly wish for your help. My trial was based on denial, not truth. While I did kill two people, I did so while seriously debilitated. Before and after the act, I maintained a stubborn pride and a deep loathing for asking for help in any way.

I was raised a Roman Catholic. This religion probably saved my life as I may have been aborted had someone not had a strong pro-life attitude. I will admit to some gratitude for this, despite my general sentiments concerning Christianity as a whole and Catholicism in particular.

My mother did my adopters no favors by not aborting me. This was part of the reason I murdered my adopters... just to make that undeniably true. I have not seen sense in that in years. I explain it to allow some insight on 'how far out there' I was. It was a way of retaliating for my abandonment... by negating my mother's 'good deed'.

Another motive was that my adopters raised me a Catholic, including the rites of Baptism and all that follows. My first and primary objection to the religious indoctrination is this: Christianity claims to have all of the answers that a human needs or should want, but it doesn't. In fact, it contradicts itself, something that the last two-thousand years of high, clever theologians spinning their apologies and polishings cannot hide from that mature mind.

Ah, but the child? A child will believe some silly things, such as that they are 'chosen,' or that they are one nationality one day, and a different one the next. My favorite lie is that I was 'reborn' to my adopters on the same day and same hour that I was born to someone else – my certified birth certificate and my Catholic baptism record say this is so, therefore it must be so. All things are possible in Catholicism.

My belief in Jesus outlived my belief in Santa Claus by several years. I understand that the common response to growing up and gaining the logic to think through one's religion is either "Don't worry about it and just hope it's true," or not to take it very seriously and just hedge your bets. Other approaches include embracing the irrational, becoming complacent upon examination of the dogma and theology, or converting to a religion one finds more acceptable, or rejecting all religions. I tried all of that and none of that worked.

I am a Pagan, not out of any desire to be peculiar nor solely to alienate myself from common doctrines, but to correct an accidental sell-out and to reconnect with my ancestors... for as their children abandoned them, so have I been abandoned.

I read *a lot*...mostly fantasy fiction with stories based in history – mostly European and ancient civilizations, philosophy – all hail Nietzche – and more general fiction like Leigh Deighton, Ed McBain and almost anything well written. I miss my computer time almost as much as I miss the company of the fairer sex. I'm an avid spectator of hockey, soccer, and football, in that order. I play role-playing games, the best known being 'Advanced Dungeons and Dragons,' and I'm working up to a play-by-mail for something to do.

There has been much speculation, following unexplained cases of children murdering children or others, as to the impact of violent television programs

Roseville couple slain before fire

Bedroom blaze set, official says

BY STEPHEN JONES,
MARTY HAIR AND ROBERT MUSIAL
Free Press Staff Writers

A Roseville couple found dead after a fire at their home were bludgeoned and slashed to death before the blaze started, the Macomb County medical examiner said Friday night.

Richard Mox, 57, and Carol Mox, 54, were in their bedroom when a flammable liquid was used to ignite their bodies, said Dr. Werner Spitz.

"They were hit on the head, their skulls were shattered," Spitz said. "Their throats were slashed. They were set on fire after they were dead."

Roseville police, who initially said they did not suspect wrongdoing in the fire, would not comment on Spitz's findings Friday night. They wouldn't discuss details of their investigation or possible suspects.

The Moxes' 21-year-old son, Gregory, a Macomb Community College student who was in the house in the 30700 block of Fernrose when the fire began, told police he was awakened by smoke and broke his bedroom window to escape.

Police questioned Gregory Mox on Friday morning but said at that time he was not a suspect.

News that the Moxes were killed before the fire turned tragedy into horror for friends and neighbors.

"We're in a state of shock here," said neighbor Martha Heika.

Joe Booza, a neighbor who had tried to enter the house to save the couple before being driven back by smoke, said neighbors "are shook up about it. There was just something that wasn't right about it."

It was Booza's house that Gregory Mox ran to for help.

He yelled, "My house is on fire and my parents are inside!" Booza said. They called 911 and went back to the Mox home but could not push through smoke, who were dead when fire fighters arrived.

Before the revelation by Spitz, friends and neighbors spoke softly of recent joys cut short by the Moxes' deaths.

Richard Mox was practicing French for his upcoming performance in "Samson and Delilah" with the Michigan Opera Theatre choir. Carol Mox had just won the chance to sing a solo with the Fraser Chorale and also had been awarded a trip to Las Vegas for being an outstanding employee.

Richard Mox had been an assembly-line worker at Ford Motor Co.'s Utica Trim plant since 1974. Carol Mox had been a receptionist at Flexys Galaxy Data Center in Troy, a data processing firm, for six years.

They moved to Fernrose Street about 26 years ago, Booza said, and raised their two daughters and son there.

Fraser Chorale director Patrick Piascentti, who directed them in the St. Joan of Arc church choir in St. Clair Shores, said they were talented musicians who loved to sing and dance, socialize and help others. Richard Mox had sung several times with Michigan Opera Theatre for more than a decade.

Carol Mox — called "Mother Mox" by coworkers for her caring ways — had won a solo in the Fraser Chorale's Mox program. She was to sing an old standard, "I Didn't Know Why."

Funeral arrangements were being made at Wasik Colasanti Funeral Home in Sterling Heights.

Jimmy Booza, a neighbor of Carol and Richard Mox, hugs friend Terry Parrish Friday as investigators comb through debris after the fatal fire.

Richard, Carol, Diane and Gregory.

17

on young minds. At the top of the list is 'Dungeons and Dragons.' Perhaps preoccupation with any form of violence is not so much a cause as a symptom.

Obviously, I'd like more college and a few vocational courses. A game company of my own was in my head, but that died in my general tumble. I could have written, but I had nothing to write about.

I like the way you write... an intense and cogent attack from page one. Truthfully, nothing I've read in years affected me as much.

"Something there is that doesn't love a wall,
that wants to tear it down,"
-Robert Frost, in "The Mending Wall"

Chapter 3:
DRUGS, DECEPTION and DENNIS KROLL

I began to hear from Greg on somewhat of a regular basis, each letter providing another chapter of his life:

"Concerning my past hospitalizations and drug history, I was treated for drug addiction, from October 1988 to June 1989 or thereabouts, at the Oxford House in Oxford, Michigan, and then at Shephard Hill in Newark, Ohio. I've had no other hospitalization of importance – just broken collarbone around 1978 and a regular series of outpatient physicals.

I was addicted to cocaine for three months in 1988, which is really strange because I never liked it. It was free at first… and why would I turn down an expensive drug? When my sister, Diane, crashed from the means by which she had been funding her drug habit, I tagged along. This was an attempt to leave the orbit of my adopters… but a wretched effort.

I like marijuana and am not averse to a strong hallucinogen every year or so. I dislike other drugs. My drug history as mentioned was my very brief stint as a coke-head, a miserable experience that I have no interest in duplicating in any way. That little chapter ended with a felony conviction for Breaking and Entering an Occupied Dwelling, my sole previous conviction for which I did a minor sentence after finishing rehab. I was not a violent man nor do I have a 'rap sheet' on hand."

Greg's admission regarding his brief cocaine addiction opened the door for me to lead him further back in his childhood. I asked him if he had another drug history – prescription drugs – such as Ritalin or Mellaril, often given to young adoptees for what was misdiagnosed in past decades as 'hyperactiveness' or Attention Deficit Hyperactive Disorder (ADHD).

"Your inquiry about prescription drugs made me recall a whole sorry set of chapters in my life. I was on LOTS of Mellaril despite that I was never hyperactive by any stretch of the imagination. I was rebellious, yes, but not 'hyper'.

It began in the sixth grade. I made a conscious decision to heckle the teacher to befriend the 'bad kids'. This was the real beginning of my enduring opposition to authority. The teacher reported my opposing attitude to her boss, the parents were informed, and I was put in child counseling... as if I wasn't already 'different' enough already, eh?

The initial belief of the counselors was that I was stupid. Why else would he be 'bad'? It didn't help that I never really tried at schoolwork. I aimed for the average to 'blend in' I think. Anyway, tests showed that I was bright, not dim. So, for reasons unknown, but probably for 'control', they settled me down with 25mg Mellaril. This didn't impress me until I saw that a really wild kid was only getting 3mg.

Counseling went on for, oh, four years, eventually involving the whole non-family. Apparently my adopter was a regular eavesdropper on my one-on-one sessions as he confronted me with something I told no one else, nowhere else. No one misses him – believe me.

Counseling was futile. Dennis Kroll of Macomb Social Services (and North American Council on Adoptable Children), became fascinated by a brick wall that I said

I felt in my brain and couldn't break through. Sometimes I called it a cloud. It was something I made up to give us something to talk about. When that finally grew stale, I just dropped it. Mr. Kroll was disappointed, no doubt, having hoped to guide me into an earth-shaking breakthrough. Too bad. All he accomplished was mellowing me out with a drug that I recall feels like marijuana, only lighter and subtler. Marijuana is my favorite drug.

I did learn how to deceive psychologists and how to lie. My adoption always set me apart but I grew uncomfortably familiar with that. I did have a huge problem with expressing emotion – especially love and anger – but I've gotten past that while locked up.

My adopters repressed emotion. Any demonstration of emotion was ridiculed by my adopter and shut down. We either said the 'proper thing' or kept quiet until we reached a constant yelling stage, ending with Diane finally moving out, and the final stage of icy silence which ended in what was in-part a mercy killing but mostly vengeance for the blight of my life."

"Adoption loss is the only trauma in the world where victims are expected by the whole of society to be grateful."
-Reverend Keith C. Griffith, MBE

Chapter 4:
ADOPTED CHILD SYNDROME

According to his article, published in 1978, *titled "Son of Sam and the Adopted Child Syndrome,"* psychotherapist and forensic psychologist, Dr. David Kirschner, upon studying adoptees, identified a pattern of eight anti-social behaviors common to "a sub-set of the spectrum" of adoptees. Harold Schecter, David M. Brodzinsky, David H. Kirk, Betty Jean Lifton, Annette Baran, Reuben Pannor, Arthur Sorosky, and other experts who treated adoptees in the course of their practice, support Kirschner's findings. The Adopted Child Syndrome (ACS) behaviors are generally described by researchers - listed below interposed with Greg Mox's observations. This author defines the 'spectrum' of adoptee behaviors as including adoptees at one end of the spectrum who cope well despite being adopted, and adoptees who cannot cope with being adopted and so develop the ACS pattern to varying degrees. The other end of the spectrum finds Greg Mox in a sudden act of violence **"without remorse."** Greg's self-descriptions, excerpted from his letters, have been matched up to all eight ACS behaviors.

- Conflict with Authority (example: truancy) –
  "I truly despise authority. I grew up a meek, obedient sort, only to realize how false and hypocritical the authority figures were. I am authority's enemy."

- Preoccupation with excessive fantasy –
  "I'm a proficient daydreamer and enjoy role-playing games which rely on the imagination. I don't 'drift off' into waking mindscapes, but I do greatly enjoy fantasizing and my sleeping dreams."

- Pathological lying –

"I lied religiously whenever I found myself in a downward spiral, including during my period of disintegration from insomnia. Diane was a master liar, a true genius at it, and I emulated her. I *did* learn how to deceive psychologists and how to lie."

- Rebelling against authority-
  Chronically angry; little or no guilt or remorse.

- Stealing –
  "I enjoyed a career as a juvenile shoplifter, feeling the toys and enjoying the rush of filching them. When that was inadequate to satisfy me, for a brief time during my cocaine use, I broke into homes."

- Running away –
  "As mentioned, I made one real attempt to run away from home when I was 18. Big deal. Sometimes I just had to GO, without knowing why, and so I went. I'm in 'general population' and have been all along, save for a few incidents such as a drug-smuggling effort, a fight, and my *escape attempt* from the county jail."

- Learning difficulties, underachiever, overachiever –
  "I was an apathetic student unless I liked the instructor. I've always been ambivalent about education due to its traditional ties to authority."

- Lack of impulse control, including sexual acting out (ranging from promiscuity to sex offenses) –
  "My sexuality is strangely normal insofar as such is possible. I'm pickier and more performance minded than most guys, mostly out of a sense of style."

- Setting fires, or enjoys arousal from fire –
  "I find fire hypnotic…soothing yet exciting…although I have no fixation for torching anyone or anything. I set their bodies on fire in an attempt to hide the evidence – not for kicks."

Twenty adoptees who murdered their adoptive families and set the houses and/or bodies on fire, such as Martin "Pyro" Pang, are detailed in Part 2 of this book. There are undoubtedly more.

These adoptees are often defiant and the act of firesetting expresses their wish to gain power and triumph over frustrating, depriving or punishing adults. The firesetting impulse is a response to the impotent **rage** they feel at a lack of control over their lives. They entertain revenge fantasies or are retaliatory in their behavior. Unless intervention is prompt and definite, these juveniles are likely to continue to set fires. The following characteristics were present most often among *"emotionally disturbed firesetters"* compared with non-firesetters.

- The presence of pleasurable or sexual excitement when lighting or watching a fire;

- Intense anger at the mother for rejecting, emotionally depriving, or abandoning the child;

- Anger at the father for being unavailable, abusive or abandoning the family, or having died;

- The tendency to respond to a narcissistic injury with rage and fantasies of revenge;

- Gaining power over adults in general by setting fires;

- Sexual conflicts or sexual dysfunction;

- Poor judgment in social situations;

- Difficulty in verbalizing anger;

Psychiatric diagnosis of "Conduct Disorder" -- about 30-40% were diagnosed with "Oppositional Disorder" or with "Conduct Disorder" with strong revenge fantasies. Open residential treatment centers are very reluctant to accept such high-risk youngsters into placement, so a specialized or highly structured correctional school would appear to offer the most appropriate placement for them. When I disclosed to Greg that he had self-described Adopted Child Syndrome behaviors, he responded:

> I have always, since age 14, been able to drop a mental root into a sea of hate as deep as the night sky. About 3 years after committing murder, I no longer reveled in hate but it remained. Ever since reading how much I am like your examples of the Adopted Child Syndrome profile, there's no hate there. Instead, I understand the *what* and the *why* of the thoughts in my head. I'm not articulating this properly, but **I feel you've given me information that would have prevented murders**. I never realized that my behavior was typical of anything, much less a fairly common reaction to the deceptive situation that my adoption has been. You could probably use the argument that silence about adoption is **reckless endangerment.** It is, after all."

And in another letter, Greg revealed:

> "I've asked many inmates about their fostering or adoptive backgrounds and the portion of inmates fostered or adopted is the larger by a fair measure. The man whose paperwork I enclosed is one such and probably more typical of prisoners than I am. He and I spoke of our mutual animosity for Catholic Social Services and I told him of you. Perhaps you can make some sense of the information he received. Another adoptee here has asked for a list of addresses for prison reformists and for prisoner pen pal services. This fellow is in constant trouble with authority."

"I'm afraid to get angry."
-Attorney Donald Humphrey, adoptee,
in "Violence in Adoption"
-American Adoption Congress Conference, 9-23-1993

Chapter 5:
TIME TO KILL

Greg didn't like talking about the murders, stating it depressed him to review that time. Abandonment issues are central in the backgrounds of adoptees who kill, including those adopted at birth and so I posed the inevitable question: Do you want to tell me what led up to the murders?

To say his response was a total surprise would be an understatement, since, in effect, he admitted premeditation:

> "At the time of the murders, I had turned 21, legally an adult. I was still living with the victims-to-be while I attended college. I do not seek to excuse my crime. My deeds were wrong and insane. The fact that I was adrift in a moral vacuum was my fault insofar as I rejected the morality imposed upon me. I murdered the closest at hand – the ones most directly involved. I am contrite but seek no forgiveness nor want any. I owe the State very little and I serve no useful purpose in prison.
>
> My adopters were quite Catholic – you know, an unwed mother is a sinner, a bastard is a child of sin. My adopter was Polish. He had brown hair, green or blue eyes – I can't recall which – and a weak chin. He was a sour and friendless man. His wife was a little Italian woman, immensely kind and slow-witted. I regret harming her.
>
> Actually, the compulsion to kill my adopter (him, not her) entered my mind the Autumn before the deed.

I resisted the impulse for six months. As I argued with myself, I lost sleep. Eventually, I would lay awake at night, staring balefully at the ceiling and also telling myself every reason *not* to do it, then trying to go about my day. This caused me to slowly fall apart. I grew duller with less and less ability to concentrate or care. Naturally, my life became tattered as I snuffed out my reasons not to do it, one by one, as my reasoning left. I made a practice of lying to cover up my decline, which of course eventually collapsed and made things far worse.

I used the word 'compulsion' deliberately. I could not rid myself of the idea because, at the root of my soul, I felt a real need to kill him for the prolonged attack he made on my very self. Killing his wife was a complete accident. My intention was only to knock her unconscious at that moment, but instead, she died. It was reckless, indeed, but not intentional.

Ultimately, I did it because I *knew* I would *eventually* do it and I would have to do it while I retained any wit at all. Telling anyone what was going on never had a chance of happening. Your timing is superb. It has only been in the past year that I've got past the entire mess sufficiently to open up about it... and, since, I feel a growing need to explain myself. An audience would therefore be handy."

Greg began to recount the events that immediately preceded the murders.

"Beginning at midnight, the night before, I laid in bed wide awake staring at the ceiling. My neck was hurting a great deal and my muscles were in knots. Sleep had been elusive not only that night but throughout the previous six months...

28

After R.J, and Carol T. Mox went to bed, the sound of Richard's snores was just one more reason to hate him that night. I listened to that mocking noise and the other 'night sounds' in the house and I oscillated from hate to fear and back to hate again. I attempted to form some plan of action but my thoughts were unruly and there was a powerful blankness. Trying to think was like painting with a dry brush.

Hours went by and Richard's alarm went off. He got up and went to work. His wife followed about an hour later. Still I remained awake. When she left, I got up. I took my time with the nothingness that it was. I went out that day and returned that evening, finding my self-appointed Parental Units asleep in the living room.

Carol awoke and, just as the night before, asked sleepily "Why didn't you call?" I could hardly say "Because keeping you and him off my mind is my last hope," so I said "I forgot." Her voice trailed after me "Dinner's in the kitchen" as she went back to sleep.

Dinner was tacos in pita bread, quickly microwaved and eaten. I scooped some ice cream into a bowl and took it into the living room to watch "Cheers." Carol managed to stay awake for most of that show, during which Richard awoke, saw me and asked his wife "Did you ask him about dinner?" "Yes," she replied. As usual. When "Amen" came on, I left. I believe I put the bowl in the sink… or maybe took it along. I read for awhile – probably one of Robert Jordan's novels, the high point of my withered day, and listened to first Carol and then Richard migrate to bed. I could tell when they were asleep. I was right back to a return of the previous night – staring at the ceiling.

About 2:00 AM, I got up and went to my closet. There, I took up my aluminum baseball bat and gripped it. The hollow bat weighed only a few pounds but could probably serve the purpose. While there's always the danger of aluminum splintering, the bat is used in little league games but deemed too dangerous for major league games due to the speed and impact of the ball. I was 'trying on' the idea of doing it and was scared how easily it fit.

I could be doing 'something' and would forever be out of the rut. The one I blamed – Richard – would be gone. For it was Richard who was sterile. In his arrogance he took in the children of others, not to love but to 'have', as he felt a man must 'have children.' The sacrifice of his wife's potential children to his need never bothered him nor her, the fool. Was she big of heart, small of brain? Both.

But to actually kill him? And what of her?

At this point of hesitation, the neighborhood's power went out. Our answering machine made its 'ooo-ooo' sound of reset and R.J. Mox woke up. Hastily, I set down the bat and met him at the end of the hallway. 'What are you doing up?' he wanted to know. 'I heard something'... 'Me, too.' He seemed pleased that we had both been awakened. A thief had been accosting the garage and had stolen some tools. I still don't know who it was but hoped to later blame him for the murders I was planning to commit. Police are not that energetic. Once they have a suspect, they're done.

So we went around checking doors and peered outside. We figured out the power outage and went back to bed. It seemed to me a sign. For half a year I had fought the idea, but just as I was about to back down, a power outage. An odd 'sign' but omens are hard to come by these days.

Suspect arrested after autopsy shows Roseville couple slain

By Ann Sweeney
THE DETROIT NEWS

Roseville police have arrested a 21-year-old man in connection with the slayings of Richard Mox, 56, and his wife, Carol Mox, 54, of Roseville.

The suspect, whose name was not released, is being held without bond in the Macomb County Jail and will be arraigned Monday in 39th District Court. Police said he will be charged with two counts of first-degree murder, and arson.

The Moxes were originally thought to be victims of a fire that raged through the bedroom of their Roseville home at 5 a.m. Friday.

An autopsy, however, revealed the couple had been bludgeoned and slashed to death before the fire.

"They were struck with a blunt instrument that smashed their skulls, and their throats were cut," said Insp. Ronald MacCool.

Their son, Gregory Mox, 21, a student at Macomb County Community College, was the only family member to escape the blaze. He told police he was awakened by the smell of smoke, and broke a window to get out.

MacCool said the fire was confined to the couple's bedroom and that a fire accelerant also had been found on the bodies, and elsewhere in the bedroom.

Richard Mox worked at Ford Motor Co.'s Utica trim plant. Carol Mox was a receptionist at FIserve Galaxy Data Center, a Troy data processing firm.

The couple had two daughters in addition to their son.

Detroit News
March 29, 1992

31

Another half hour passed.

Without the slightest hesitation, I took up the bat and rushed to their bedroom. I hit him once in the forehead, a soft, wet, smacking sound.

Carol bolted upright, drawing in a startled breath. I was overcome with the horror of her seeing me harm her husband and hit her about a third as hard to knock her out. She stopped breathing. I discovered she had died instantly.

But her husband still breathed. I hit him a dozen more times. *Still* he breathed. Why, when the 'good one' died so easily, did the one I hated live on? Finally, I decided to let him suffer. I hit Carol's corpse a few more times *to make the damage look even* but couldn't bear to continue it. None of it was loud.

I turned on the light and discovered blood streaks across the ceiling and droplets of blood were splattered everywhere. I looked at Carol – what remained of her – and had all the remorse a man could ask for.

Then I showered, taking the bat along and taking the kitchen phone off the hook because R.J. *still* continued breathing and might have had a 911 call left in him.

In the shower, I recovered somewhat. My overwhelming emotion was numb with disgust. After washing myself twice and the bat thrice, I got fresh clothing and went downstairs. There, I put the bloody clothing in the washer and returned to check on the victims while the washer went through its cycles.

Richard was obviously dying. I left him to it. I made an attempt to clean up and realized it was not going to happen. Blood was on the ceiling, on the walls, on the furniture, seeping through the mattress and the carpet.

I decided the only solution was fire.

Accelerants were probably totally unnecessary but I used them anyway. Despite going to great trouble not to use the gas cans in the garage, the police later claimed I did. There were cans of gasoline in the basement. I used a little of that. I wasn't thinking right and was in the giddiness of unreality. It was more comfortable that way.

I placed the bat with the other sports equipment in the basement where it went unnoticed by the police. For some reason, they chose to believe I tore a shelf off the wall of their bedroom and hit them with that. That shelf had actually been knocked off the wall with one of my swings at Richard.

Some gas on the bedroom floor and out came some matches. I lit the corner of the mattress. I was dumbly astonished at how quickly it all went up. On the way out, I took down the cross at the end of the hallway, went out and threw it into the garbage can at the curb.

Then I returned to my bedroom, door open, and stared at the ceiling for the last time. I patiently waited for some smoke to be visible before leaving.

I then waited in the van parked in front of the house for the fire to progress. But a passing driver saw the smoke, slowed at the cross-street for a good look, and sped off. I had to beat him to make the first call to 911 and begin my act as innocent bystander.

At about 7:00 am, I was at the Booza's house, diagonally across the street from my house. I had run over there, appropriately distraught, to call for help since their light was on.

Fire suspect called loner, 'real clever'

BY JEFFREY S. GHANNAM
Free Press Staff Writer

To neighbors in Roseville, Gregory Mox is a quiet computer whiz.

But to police and prosecutors in Macomb County, Mox, 21, is the main suspect in the gruesome deaths of his parents, Richard and Carol Mox.

"Something must have snapped," said the Rev. Arthur Fauser of Our Lady Queen of All Saints Catholic Church in Fraser, which the Mox family has attended since 1964. "I feel sorry for him. I've never seen him a violent guy. He's a gentle person."

The Moxes — Richard, 57 and Carol, 54 — were pulled early Friday

Richard Mox and Carol Mox, with son Gregory and daughter Diane smile in a family portrait years ago. Gregory, now 21, is accused of killing and setting his parents and their Roseville home on fire.

from their burned home in the 30700 block of Ferntree. An autopsy showed the couple had been killed and their bodies doused with a flammable liquid and set afire.

Macomb County Prosecutor Carl Marlinga said Sunday that his office has requested a warrant charging Gregory Mox with two counts of open murder and one count of arson.

Mox is expected to be formally arraigned on the charges today in 39th District Court in Roseville. If convicted, Mox would face mandatory life in prison with no chance for parole.

Police declined to speculate on a motive.

Mox was taken into police custody late Friday and spent the weekend in

See SUSPECT, Page **5B**

Detroit Free Press,
Monday, March 30, 1992, Metro, p9

Cops say son killed parents

Murder, arson charged in deaths

BY JEFFREY S. GHANNAM
Free Press Staff Writer

About a month ago, Gregory Mox told a friend that he wanted to kill his parents, police said Monday as Mox was arraigned in the brutal slayings of his parents.

Richard Mox, 57, and Carol Mox, 54, were bludgeoned and slashed to death early Friday before being doused with gasoline and set afire in the bedroom of their Roseville home, authorities said.

Gregory Mox, 21, was charged in 39th District Court with two counts of open murder and one count of arson. He was ordered to be held in the Macomb County Jail without bond until his preliminary examination on April 8.

Without giving details, Roseville Police Detective John Sarrach told Judge William Ward: "The defendant threatened to kill his parents."

Police wouldn't discuss the context in which the alleged threat was made. "We don't know if a motive at this point," said Roseville Lt. Joseph Steenland.

Outside court, Mox's sisters, Christine Marchione and Diane Theis, wouldn't comment.

According to Macomb County Circuit Court files, Mox had earlier brushes with authorities. The records show he was treated for a chemical dependency at two inpatient substance abuse programs, starting in 1984.

Mox also pleaded guilty in March 1989 to an attempted break-in of an occupied house in St. Clair Shores in October 1988. He was sentenced in April 1989 to three years probation and served the first six months in the Macomb

County Jail.

As part of his probation, Mox was to continue substance abuse treatment. He was released from probation in April 1991.

Mox has attended Macomb County Community College since late 1989. This semester, he was enrolled in introduction to philosophy, beginning French and computer principles courses. Until six months ago, he worked for DialAmerica, a telemarketing service in Troy, but was seventh unemployed, said his friend, Justine Hartmann of Clinton Township.

"This guy is brilliant," said Hartmann, who worked with Mox at DialAmerica. "He lived on his computer. He's a good person, very caring."

Hartmann said Mox called her from the jail on Sunday and said: "Justine, one thing I want you to do is help me find out what really happened to my parents."

Police said Gregory Mox arrived at his parents' brick bungalow on Ferntree Street about 11:20 p.m. Thursday.

His parents were upset with him for staying out the night before, Roseville detective Sarrach said. "He was out and they didn't

know where he was."

Mox told police he went to sleep and was awakened about 5 a.m. by smoke. He told police he escaped by breaking a window in his bedroom.

Neighbor Joe Booda has said Mox came to his home yelling for help, wearing slippers, pajamas and a bathrobe.

"He said he couldn't get in the house, but he had his keys in his pocket. There was just something that wasn't right about it. The police asked him about the keys, but he said he always kept his keys in his bathrobe pocket," Booda said.

Gregory Mox is arraigned Monday in 39th District Court with two counts of open murder and one count of arson in the brutal slayings of his parents at their Roseville home last Friday.

Detroit Free Press,
Tuesday, March 31, 1992, Metro, p3

I knew the Parishes next door but the house was dark and they were frequently out of town. I sat in their house trying to think while the Booza's tried to comfort me. Thereafter, the Booza's house became the 'command center' of the police and fire departments as I listened in on their conversations.

What the police latched onto was my 'gray rolling mist' story. Unknown to me, my room had no smoke damage. Since I hadn't left until *I actually did see smoke*, I knew they were wrong to claim I could not have seen smoke. But they later 'proved' me a liar with their 'expert.'

By 4:00 pm the same day, everyone in the family was gathered at the house directly across the street from my adopters' house. This meeting spot was the home of Joan and John Parish, a couple who had grown up with my nominal parents. The police were finishing up their dissection of the crime scene and Diane and I, along with the Parish's daughter, Terry, who had returned from the airport with Christina, were watching the coverage and commiserating glumly when Christina reported that the police were coming over.

From the beginning, both detectives, Sarrach and Urianiak, stared at me – especially Urianiak while Sarrach was doing the talking. They were so clearly trying to unnerve me that I felt contemptuous of them, which was a mistake. In my unbalanced state, I felt over-confident. They asked me to come down to the station. Christina immediately came to my rescue saying that since I wasn't under arrest, I need not go anywhere with them. Sarrach responded "We can put him under arrest. In fact, he is" and out came the handcuffs. I was taken out to their patrol car and I've been locked up ever since.

Oh – my one phone call. It was to Diane."

GETTING IT STRAIGHT

The Free Press corrects all errors of fact. If you know of an error, please call Charlotte Craig, assistant to the executive editor, at 222-2441 or 1-800-678-7771 anytime. Or write her at 321 W. Lafayette, Detroit 48226.

■ A Tuesday article about the arraignment of Gregory Mox, 21, of Roseville in the deaths of his parents should have said he was charged with two counts of first-degree murder.

Detroit Free Press,
Wednesday, April 1, 1992

MACOMB

Son, 21, to stand trial in deaths of parents

ROSEVILLE — A 21-year-old man was ordered Monday to stand trial on first-degree murder and arson charges in the slayings of his parents.

Gregory Mox, who is being held without bond, is accused of bludgeoning and slashing Richard, 57, and Carol, 54, before setting their Roseville home on fire March 26.

Slaying suspect to get competency hearing

ROSEVILLE — A judge on Wednesday ordered tests to determine whether a Roseville man is competent to stand trial for the slayings of his parents.

Gregory Mox, 21, is charged with first-degree murder and arson in the March 27 deaths of Richard Mox, 57, and Carol Mox, 54. They were bludgeoned and slashed to death and set afire.

Chapter 6:
THE TRIAL

"During the pre-trial buildup, I signed waivers for everything in my parents' estate to diminish my motive. Still, the will came up in the trial but not my waiving it. After my conviction, the insurance company still notified me that I was getting nothing. I didn't care then and I don't care now.

Diane was quite caught up in the drama of it all and clearly set about assuming responsibility as matriarch of the family. Chris was quiet and observant but also and rather forceful at times when obstructed by authorities.

Other than one pretty woman I recall fondly; I do not recall much about the jury. Their names are recorded in the "voire dire" form from my trial in my transcripts. My lawyer looked like Dr. Johnny Fever in the old "WKRP in Cincinnati" TV show. I believe he blew my trial purposely and I hate him for it. The prosecutor, Steven Caplan, is a dinky little man who recently ran for Chief Prosecutor of a county neighboring Macomb and lost. One day I will have to have a little chat with him but I understand that he was just doing his job. The Honorable George Steeh is a mild fellow who gave me something like a fair trial."

Prosecutors theorized that Greg and his parents were at odds over the lifestyle he had been living. The night proceeding the slayings, the elder Mox and his adopted son argued over Greg having been

41

out all day without telephoning his whereabouts.

> The Prosecution made much of the garbage cans at the curb. Apparently, it being trash day, the sanitation engineers removed our garbage as scheduled, despite the police cars, fire engine, news truck and all the circus. The Prosecution implied that all manner of evidence they needed had gone into those cans when only that cross, the symbol of everything I grew to hate, was so disposed.

> The expert witness swore there was no smoke in my room, which was a lie. The reason there wasn't anything like the smoke damage to the rest of the house was due to the unintended consequence of my having opened the front door when I threw out the cross. That drew in the air in such a way that it slammed the door of my room shut, preventing dirtier smoke from getting in.

> My defense was essentially 'I saw nothing and heard nothing', which my lawyer told me 'only had a chance' if I testified. Then he made a deal with the Prosecutor – without consulting me – insuring that I would not testify.

> So, because I was 'lying' to him by insisting that I killed them 'for no reason,' he threw my defense."

On May 31, 1995, the Michigan Court of Appeals upheld the two 1993 First Degree Premeditated Murder and Arson convictions against Gregory Mox.

Man convicted of killing parents

MT. CLEMENS — Gregory Mox, 22, of Roseville was convicted Tuesday of bludgeoning his parents, dousing their bodies with gasoline and setting them on fire at their home in March 1992.

After more than nine hours of deliberations, a Macomb County Circuit Court jury found Mox guilty of first-degree murder and arson in the deaths of his father, Richard Mox, 57, and mother, Carol Mox, 54.

Before the killings, Mox — a Macomb Community College student at the time — had argued with his parents over staying out late. Richard Mox had restricted his son's computer use, prosecutors said.

Detroit Free Press, 1993

43

*"Adoptees always have these questions.
When you're all grown up can't you know who you are?"*
-Coco Brush, birth mother, founder of 'ANSWERS"

Chapter 7:
THE SEARCH and "SISTER" ALES

I had promised Greg that I would pursue whatever I needed to do to locate his birth family... and to maintain confidentiality in course of searching according to the wishes of all who may become involved. I had nothing to go on but his adoptive name and alleged birth date. We had nothing on his parents – not ages nor backgrounds. We did not know if he had siblings. As adoptees often do, Greg wondered whether he might have bumped into a sibling without knowing and whether his criminality was 'genetic," apparent when Greg wrote:

> "There's an 18-year old named Privacky who quite resembles me – tall, thin, pale, glasses, killed his parents – right here in Muskegon County. He's just been sentenced after pleading 'no contest' to four counts of First Degree Murder and is in either Muskegon County Jail or Riverside Quarantine of the Michigan Department of Corrections... I don't know if he's adopted but I suspect some connection to me. He really looks a lot like I did ten years ago and I hope you will inquire after him."

Coincidentally, Greg does bear an eerie resemblance to Seth Privacky who, on November 29, 1998, murdered five people during Thanksgiving dinner: his father, his 'father's wife' (as she is described in news clips), his grandfather, his brother, and his brother's girlfriend, who had unfortunately stopped by after Seth had murdered his family. Seth shot each of his victims in the head, execution style. Crying, as he often did following arguments with his father, Seth phoned his friend, 18-year old Steven Wallace, saying he had "made a big mistake" and got Wallace to come over without explanation. Fearing for his life, Wallace was enlisted to help move the bodies.

Seth Privacky   *Greg Mox*

Privacky pleaded 'no contest' and on May 1999 was sentenced to Life in prison. Charges against Wallace were dismissed. If Greg Mox and Seth Privacky have any connection, it may be the fact that they didn't get along with the men who raised them, and both apparently had lost their natural mother. Seth had been taking prescribed anti-depressant medication at the time of the killing spree and at an earlier time in his life he had been on Mellaril, had been smoking marijuana, and, just as Greg claimed, he, too, suffered a long-term sleep deficit at the time of the murders. In both cases, the unintended victims (Seth's brother's girlfriend and Greg's adoptive mother) happened to get in the way – collateral damage -- during their sudden, uncontrollable **rage**.

Like Noah Stone (in "8 Ball Cafe"), who had always sensed he 'had a brother somewhere' (and we *did* later discover a brother he could not have known about), Greg may intuitively be seeking his unknown sibling. But, like many adoptees who believe that they are a "bad seed," Greg was looking for the face of a "parent killer."

On August 23, 2000, at Greg's suggestion, I wrote to Attorney Mark. S. Kistner, Jr., requesting a copy of Greg's trial transcripts and various records, using Greg's signed authorization. I also asked "Do you recall whether there was any attempt to discover and contact Greg's biological mother prior to the trial?" There was no reply.

On May 5, 1999, an acknowledgement from Maureen Spitzley, Secretary of the Adoption Services Division of Michigan's Family Independence Agency (FIA), which is their name for Social Services, was sent to Greg c/o my PO Box in reply to his request for information regarding location of his adoption records. A May 14, 1999 follow-up letter from FIA could not even confirm that Greg was adopted, let alone from what Michigan agency. Neither did the letter invite Greg to file appropriate forms to list him on their state reunion registry, but it was suggested he might contact the Family Division of Macomb County Circuit Court at Mt. Clemmens.

The Macomb County Circuit Court also replied-- by identifying the adoption agency as being Catholic Services of Macomb.

Logic suggested we then also had the court that holds Greg's adoption file, including the Final Decree of Adoption, but neither the court nor Catholic Services would admit to it.

On June 4, 1999, the Department of Community Health and Consumer Services, at Lansing, returned my letter signed by Greg, requesting the name and location of the court where his adoption occurred and the hospital where he was born. The response to both requests, on a pink Post-It note said simply "need a court order to process." But on July 13, 1999, Greg received a form letter from Joanne Ales, Catholic Services of Macomb, outlining what the agency could and could not provide under present Michigan statues. Traditionally Catholic adoption agency social workers were Catholic nuns, and so we referred to her as "Sister" Ales.

At the same time, I heard back from a woman named Jan who was seeking the son she gave up for adoption. Initially, her information seemed it could be a 'match.' Although she proved not to be Greg's biological mother, she gave Greg a new perspective about 'birth' mothers. Jan wrote:

> "I would like to contact this young man. I have many questions about what it's like being a 30-year old man who doesn't know his parents. I suspect I could share insights he'd like to know also. I don't have any sources for more information, but will try to help if I can. Please forward my information to him and thanks so much for all the good work you are doing. My emotions run the gamut on my search. As much as I want to find my son, I have a deep-seated belief that I don't have the right to barge into his life. Of course, on my 'aggressive' days I spend hours combing the web, newspapers, phone directories, etc. I guess we all have to be a bit crazy after all we've been through. Again, I look forward to hearing from him.
>
> –Jan"

Greg responded: "Although it seems improbable, I'd certainly like Jan to be my mother."

Greg enclosed a letter to Jan for me to forward to her:

"Thank you for your kind interest! I hope you find your son. I agree I'm probably not he, but one look at his photograph or a reproduction of it will resolve that. Whether or not, I will be happy to answer any questions you care to pose.

I'd like to know what adoption is like from the other end. What brought you to give up your son? When did you begin to search for him? I don't wish to trample your emotions, having found my own quite volatile on the subject.

So [you ask] what's it like being a 30-year old man who doesn't know his parents? It is... peculiar. Having never known another state, I am adjusted to it. The problem is subtle, really. People have families, except I don't. The family I was adopted into was really a group of strangers, like a short-line at the checkout counter, forced to live in one house for years. Even families that don't get along have a bond, a flow of mutual understanding that I saw in other families but never felt myself. It was like being half-human.

Why have I waited so long? Pride, mostly. It's a complicated thing to explain. There is a certain resentment at being abandoned, certainly. I dealt with that by rejecting the search notion – turning my back on the family that had done that to me. I also had plans of becoming a great success, so as to be able to look down on my family-politely, of course. Perhaps this strikes you as immature. It certainly strikes me that way.

What you may like to know is that I have known many adoptees and not a one wouldn't welcome the chance to meet their mother. Perhaps others feel more emotional support from their adopters than I did, but there is a place no other can fill. I pray your search is successful and wish you well in all things. I hope to get word from you again and shall close for now.

-Sincerely,
Gregory Mox"

Greg was enthused by the prospect of broadening contacts throughout the World Wide Web to assist his search. He had been learning the versatility of his own computer just before the murders. But hope faded into the reality that not only was Jan not his mother but also most mothers are not informed of law changes since they relinquished their children and so probably most did not know about registries and possibilities for contact with their adult children within or outside the system. Neither did we have a clue as to whether Greg's mother *wanted* to be found.

One Michigan searcher informed me that one reason no one could "sell" Greg a search is that **no one had 1970 birth indexes** that could possibly reveal Greg's birth name and/or his parents' names. Consequently, **no one had the information to sell**, as was commonly done in other states and even by county governments (for instance, Ohio's local government agencies sold birth indexes for the year needed... and Texas birth indexes were available for a time). This was decades before "DNA searches."

On January 14, 2000, Joanne Ales, Catholic Services of Macomb, replied to Greg:

"Dear Mr. Mox,

We are in receipt of your request for non-identifying information. From previous information we have received, it is our understanding that you are incarcerated in the State of Michigan and not California.

Joanne Ales, MSW, ACSW,
married 32 years,
described as a "pro life social worker" 30 years,
specializing in adoption
as the "Macomb County Adoption Specialist."
She died at age 74 in 2016

Due to these circumstances, we are returning to Lori Carangelo the check she issued in the amount of $60. We will be happy to provide the requested information directly to you upon the request from you directly. We will need your signed request, a check in the amount of $60 and a new signed Consent Form.

-Sincerely,
Joanne G. Ales, ACSW, Director of Child Welfare"

I immediately phoned Joanne Ales who then made comments about prisoners that suggested her bias. She not only refused to waive either her $60 fee for "non-identifying information," or her non-refundable $250 fee to act as "Confidential Intermediary," a conflict of interest since she also held his adoption file and an limit any information in it that may paint the agency in a bad light, but also insisted that "*prisoners can get money.*" Greg felt it would probably be a waste of money since it seemed she did not intend to disclose anything to Greg.

In February, 2000, Greg forwarded a request for assistance to Clayton D. Burch, the Prisoner Ombudsman at the Office of Legislative Corrections in Lansing. Greg asked Burch to act as a Confidential Intermediary or to help Greg obtain a neutral intermediary, for the purpose of obtaining his non-identifying pre-adoption background information, including any family medical information, and a waiver of the usual fee CI of $250 or more. The request was denied on the grounds that Greg "had not exhausted all other legal avenues."

On May 19, 2000, I mailed Greg's notarized letter-petition, by certified return-receipt mail (because he said he could not return-receipt it from prison) to the Honorable Pamela Gilbert O'Sullivan, Judge of the State Probate Court, Juvenile Division, County of Macomb, at Mt. Clemens, Michigan:

RE: RENEWED REQUEST FOR IDENTITY OF
           COURT OF JURISDICTION IN THE MATTER
           OF MY ADOPTION, AND:

1) APPEAL for Court Order Compelling Release of my non-identifying medical or other background information from agency and court files to treat adoptee and to verify legality of adoption (because of DENIALS by agency) per this Court's discretion to do so;

2) REQUEST for Court Appointed Confidential Intermediary (enclosed) to be paid by the Court's Pro Bono Funds, and for Waiver of Court fees, or, in the alternative;

3) REQUEST for Order to Release Original Pre-Adoption Birth Certificate, Petition to Adopt and/or Final Decree of Adoption, unblocked.

I provided my Affidavit verifying the allegations in Greg's letter-petition about which I had direct knowledge. All we could do then was wait. In the meantime, Greg contemplated requesting a Governor's pardon:

"Perhaps I should promise Engler that, if he pardons me, *I'll only kill Democrats.* I suspect he has a list… (yes, that's a joke)."

June 30, 2000:
"Administration was told that I was going to have someone come here and 'kill guard's so that so I could escape. I now understand their intense reaction, although I'm not sanguine about the way they trampled on my rights in the hearing process. Fortunately, I had that off-site visit – a premium opportunity for escape – and one I knew of well beforehand. It demonstrated that, had I the inclination, and outside help, I could have been gone, without more murder or any conspirators. I also have two psychologists telling me I *was* psychotic, but am no longer, nor have I been for years. One advised me not to have any dealing with you. Too bad.

Chapter 8:
"FORGET THE WHOLE THING"

"He came to my cell door here in administrative segregation and opened the food slot at the three-foot from ground level to talk through it. This is fairly typical practice, although, the previous psychiatrist brought me into a room for private discussion. Talking through a food slot can be overheard by about 30 other inmates which can lead to my current predicament. If any rat-type inmate has some relevant information on someone, they can easily work up useful, believable lies based on overheard information. Previously, I didn't give a damn, but this fiasco since June 5 has made me not so cavalier.

So he squatted down to face me through the slot and said: 'Mr. Mox, I'm here to discuss your psychiatric health request.'

I hopped down from my bunk and said 'Great!' First of all, I'm not suicidal, no bam-bam room for me, please." This is in reference to the suicide watch cell and the issues attire which resembles the outfit of Bam-Bam on the Flintstones.

'Well, I'm glad to hear that,' he replied. He then gave me the standard pep talk for inmates which he had to do. This is heartwarming Dale Carnegie but focused on encouraging the troubled inmate finding some way of making a positive contribution to society despite the difficulties of being a prisoner.

After that, he got around to asking what made me seek counseling.

I explained that I was in prison for murdering my adoptive parents and am serving Life ... and then had to endure his 'Lifer' version of the pep talk. I had already heard both, two days earlier, so I interrupted with "I'm alright about being in prison. I wrote about the mental health breakdown that put me in here. I gave him a rundown of the insomnia and irrationality of that time and the depression I get when thinking back to it. He seized on the depression.

'If it breaks you up to dwell on the past, that part of the past, then don't do it. You're absolutely not psychotic anymore.'

I thought that was a quick diagnosis, if a welcome one, and he didn't suggest I was paranoid. In my health service request, I complained of paranoia and being psychotic at the time of my crime. I went on to explain the necessity of going through that time, in the interest of getting my story published, explaining how I screwed up, and why. This, he did not like, and asked Are you writing the book yourself?' I said 'No, I don't want to. It's all I can do to provide material to this activist in California.' I could write it up well enough myself except I find it too depressing to go back there in my mind. I doubt how objective I could be, too, since the whole incident is so humiliating that I would have to try to brighten things up.

'So why is this person out-of-state writing your story? If dredging up all this is painful for you, you should just leave it alone. We don't offer one-on-one therapy here. It can't be good to put yourself through it all again. It sounds to me like the person wants to exploit you to further humiliation. I advise you to have nothing to do with him."

'*Her,*' I corrected him.

'Her. Have nothing to do with her and forget the whole thing.'

It's a bit late for that and I don't agree. My story could do others some good and I'm beyond the whole public humiliation thing; that was years ago. What I wanted to talk to you about was making sure I'm not going to go off and kill anyone ever again. I mean, I don't think I am, but it kind of snuck up on me the first time, you know?"

I don't think you need to worry about that. I can tell you're not psychotic. *It seems to me you were suffering from diminished capacity at the time.*'

Well, duh. After that, he made his exit speech and left. I've decided to wait until I'm at a better facility to seek meaningful help.

By October, Greg was moved out of segregation but was still in a high level of security despite that he was cleared of all allegations that had landed him there. He indicated he expected to be moved to a minimum security facility some time in 2001. Because I have never seen any of the prison's documentation about the allegations, investigation, and findings, I could only wonder whether Greg actually had unsuccessfully attempted an escape but was successful at 'running a game' on prison officials as they claimed.

Chapter 9:
DIGGING UP and BURYING THE PAST

I wanted to know more about Greg's adoptive sisters and what they could tell me about Greg and all three adoptions. I wondered if they had since found, or been found by, their biological families or whether they received the same treatment by Catholic Services. I didn't mind spinning my wheels if it turned out that Greg's sisters preferred to 'bury the past' than talk about it, but it troubled me that Greg had omitted mentioning how and when Christina had been in contact with him through attorney Kistner. I needed to know, before approaching his sisters or Kistner, whether they had simply parted ways or whether they feared risking Greg knowing their whereabouts, although Greg stated their adoptive parents were not liked by his adoptive siblings either.

> "Diane is nobody to me. I never loved her. She received some information about her family but evidently did nothing about it. She is three years my senior and Christina is three years older than her. She was just a kid herself with her own problems.
>
> Diane used me as a toy. I don't believe it should be called abuse, though the games ranged from cute to terrifying. When I was five, and she was eight, she once cornered me in the back of the garage with a pitchfork. I fully believed she was serious in her chanted promises to impale me and nail me to the wall so I couldn't get help. I grabbed a shovel with both hands and tried my best to chop her head in two. She still has a scar on her forehead. She gave me some space for awhile after that. I was impressed by how seriously I was punished for it. If Diane had not been able to neatly slither around my explanation for having been driven to the act, I might

59

have better accepted being grounded, but I was punished while Diane was fussed over. I hated my adopters then, and Diane as well, and I tried to run away. I had a vague fantasy of finding another family to move in with, but I didn't get any farther than the second corner, disappointed and bewildered.

Diane was a masterful liar, as far back as I can remember. One of my first memories, before I could walk or talk, was hearing 'Chris good, Diane bad.' One of her standard responses to such parental chastisement or anger was to misdirect it.

They stifled my soul and people expect me to forgive that because they didn't otherwise abuse me? It seems they never notice you exist unless you're in trouble or on display.

I do love Chris, but she's lost touch for some reason the past two years.

All three of us were adopted from Catholic Social Services of Macomb County. You're welcome to contact Diane, who I last heard was divorced, but I'm not really interested. We were not close. I'm not sure what, if anything, she felt for Carol Mox, but, like Chris and me, she disliked Richard. She was married at the time of the murders and was forced to reveal an affair to account for her presence that night, which still amuses me a bit. She visited me regularly and added money to my account, until I was convicted. After my conviction, 'snip-snip."

I had been trying to locate Greg's adoptive sisters, Christina and Diane, via nationwide public directory listings online and letters to all by the same name. There were no replies.

Acting on a lead from Diane's ex-husband, I phoned a number and asked Diane's son if he knew how I could reach his mother who I

60

identified by one of her previous married names. The young man corrected me, stating that was her previous name and supplying the other name as her current name. He wanted to know what it was about but I just assured him I wasn't a bill collector and that it wasn't bad news.

After he gave me her home number, I hesitated. It occurred to me that if Diane had successfully buried her past, she probably didn't want to be found. But on the chance that she could provide even one missing piece to Greg's puzzle, I made the call.

The woman who answered was quite pleasant, but when I asked if she was Greg Mox's adoptive sister, she insisted I had the" wrong Diane." I tried assuring her that I had not told her son my specific reason for my call and that our conversation would be kept confidential. I further explained that I hoped to help Greg locate his family and asked whether she had ever located her family. She denied that she was adopted and informed me there was another Diane by the same last name in the same state. I apologized for the wrong number and after a minute of polite chat, we hung up.

Then it dawned on me that there could not be two Dianes with a husband and son by the same last names, as well as having the same prior married name according to the ex-husband and son. An adoptee, Janette Winterson, shared the following insight

> "Adopted children are *self-invented* because we have to
> be; there is an absence, a void, a question mark at the
> very beginning of our lives."

Had I found Diane? Or one of her split selves? I decided not to disturb her past and present lives so well hidden.

When last I heard from Greg, he had not renewed his request for his pre-adoption background information nor for contact with his mother, despite that "Sister" Ales was then retired. Perhaps as a last desperate effort to find new basis for Appeal, or as an escape from the harshness of reality, Greg alleged that it wasn't he who murdered his adoptive parents -- that he was actually *protecting Diane.*

Chapter 10:
GREG MOX TODAY

Greg Mox, age 48 in 2018

At this writing, Gregory Mox, MDOC prisoner # 231008, remains incarcerated at Michigan's Lakeland Correctional Facility for the 1992 murders of his adoptive parents when he was 21. He has been in prison 26 years -- more than half his life -- his 2006 Petition for Writ of Certiorari Denied by the United States Supreme Court.

In April 2012, the *Detroit Free Press* focused on another Michigan adoptee who committed parricide - Tucker Cipriano, 19.

Tucker Cipriano, age 19 in 2012

Tucker Cipriano, while high on drugs, bludgeoned his adoptive parents with the same weapon of choice – a baseball bat - succeeding in killing his adoptive father, Robert Cipriano. His adoptive mother, Rosemary Cipriano, and their 17-year old biological son, Salvatore, were critically injured from the attack but survived. In the months leading up to the attack, according to his own Facebook postings, Tucker had become preoccupied with the fact that he is adopted. A friend of his informed media that Tucker's birth mother had recently died – which is when Tucker "went off the deep end." Described by neighbors as a "basically nice kid," Tucker was emotionless at the time of his arrest and described as *'unremorseful'*.

The "experts" speculated that Tucker must be '"wired wrong" from "bad genes," never questioning how he *felt* about being adopted and his need to know about his birth family. His adoptive relatives persuaded him to plead "No Contest"' to avoid a trial that could have answered the same question that police and media had similarly asked about the Greg Mox murders: **"Why?"**

Greg Mox's prison psychiatrist, who was not adoption-oriented, attempted to dissuade Greg from publishing his story and "just forget the whole thing," apparently not comprehending the effect of lifelong submissiveness to the 'don't ask, don't tell' rules of adoption that ked to his crime. And shouldn't Greg's adoptive parents, who religiously monitored his comings and goings, have noticed descent into depression and understood his and his adoptive siblings' need to know about their origins?

Jean Paton, social worker, open records activist, herself an adoptee, commented:

"Do you have to be truant, steal cars, get into juvenile detention homes, take drugs, drop out of school – [and we might add, 'kill your adoptive parents'] – in order for people to realize that you need to have someone tell you about your origins?"

Apparently the answer is still *'Yes.'*

PART 2:
HOW OTHER ADOPTIONS IGNITED A FIRE

**13% of 69 firesetters were adopted,
compared to a control group of non-firesetters,
3% of whom were not adopted.**

(Source: Dr Wayne S Wooden and Dr. Martha Lee Berkey, *"Study of
Youthful Firesetters in the San Bernardino County,
California Juvenile Justice System"*)

Adopted serial killers who were prolific pyromaniacs
include David Berkowitz (1,411 fires) and Joseph Kalinger.

CHARLES BOCOOK, 15,
and GLADYS BOCOOK, 14

Charles Bocook, 15, and his biological sister, Gladys Bocook, were born to Melody Workman of Sardinia, Ohio. In 1992, after their biological father had been jailed, Melody Workman relinquished them for adoption to Charles and Gladys Bocook who re-named the children after themselves.

The teenagers planned to kill their adoptive parents *so they could return to their biological mother, Melody.*

They waited for the Bocooks to fall asleep in their mobile home in Sardinia before igniting the house afire and fleeing in their adoptive parents' car. They kept going until they reached their mother's house in McArthur, Ohio, about 2 hours away. Their adoptive parents were injured in the fire but managed to escape through a window. Charles Bocook, 67, managed to pull his wife, Gladys, 52, to safety and she was treated for burns to her back and arms and smoke inhalation. The teenagers were tried as adults for Aggravated Arson and Attempted Murder.

(--Source: *"Siblings To Be Sentenced for Attempted Murder of Adoptive Parents,"* AP, 11-14-00)

ROBERT OTIS COULSON, 24

Born 3-11-68 in Rhode Island, the redheaded Coulson and his siblings were adopted in Texas. Coulson completed 14 years of school and worked in sales. When Coulson was 24 he was convicted of the 11-13-92 murders of Robin and Robert Wentworth, 2 of 5 adoptive family members, including his adoptive parents who he killed allegedly for inheritance, by tying them up with plastic flex cuffs and suffocating them with plastic bags taped over their heads.

He then doused the bodies and house with gasoline and ignited a fire in an effort to cover his crime.

Coulson's natural father wrote to the Texas Board of Pardons and Paroles asking that his son be spared from execution. *He also told of the 'guilt' he has felt over the years for allowing his children to be put up for adoption, blaming Texas for pushing him to do so.*
"(--Source: Robert Anthony Phillips, *"The Death House,"* Death Penalty News; Texas Criminal Justice Offender Information website)

MARTIN PANG, 39

Martin Pang was born in 1955 in Hong Kong, as Sun Hing Wah, and adopted by Mary and Harry Pang when he was 6 months old. Rice Pang, Martin's third of his 4 ex-wives, told the ATF that she had been alerted by two of Martin's friends who he had approached about murdering her after their 1986 divorce, and also talked about murdering his wealthy adoptive parents. Rice said he beat her, threatened her with firearms and once kicked her in her stomach while she was pregnant, endangering the life of their baby.

Since 1994, Martin Pang began to share with friends his idea of burning down his adoptive parents' warehouse of and finding a way of having them die together in a fire because of a double indemnity clause in their $1-million dollar insurance. The Pangs had grown their little start-up frozen-food operation in the Chinatown section of Seattle into a million-dollar business, doling out much of the profit to nurture bar-hopping womanizing Martin with speedboats, Porsches, exotic vacations, from a generous allowance the Pangs extended to their adopted son.

He had contacted his parents' attorney in an attempt to read their will to determine what his split might be should they die. Mary Pang had shown Martin their will, fearful that he'd get angry if she refused. He also discussed maybe having their car blow up. It didn't stay quiet for long.

In 1998, dubbed by media as "Pyro" Pang, he pled Guilty to 4 counts of Manslaughter to avoid a Life sentence in deaths of 4 firefighters resulting from the Arson fire he set with the intention of killing his wife and his adoptive parents

Although the Pangs were unharmed by the fire, Harry Pang's health began to fail following the arson and he died at age 83 in 2004; Mary Pang died at age 87 in 2009.

(--Source: *"Martin Pang: Burning Man,"* Seattle Weekly News, 12-18-12)

Drifter Charged
In Bludgeoning
Of His Parents

A Connecticut Couple Is
Found Dead in Yard

Patrick Campbell after his arrest yesterday in Kent, Conn.

PATRICK K. CAMPBELL, 20

Patrick Campbell was born in Michigan, in 1967, one of 5 children who was first given to foster parents with whom he had developed bonds. When he was 16 months old, the platinum haired, blue eyed baby boy, was adopted by Kenneth M. Campbell, a stock broker, and his wife, Anna May Campbell. Patrick said "I never got along with my adoptive parents all my life. We were always fighting. They favored my [adoptive] sister, Jill, not me." Jill, said he seemed disoriented in his new home.

In 1997, at age 20, Patrick killed his adoptive father, 56, and his adoptive mother, 59 – by bludgeoning them to death, with an axe and sledgehammer in the basement of their Farmington, Connecticut, home, **and set the basement stairwell on fire, hoping to cover up the murders. When the fire went out, he dragged their bodies to a wooded are in back of the house, doused their bodies with gasoline and set them on fire,** then drove off in their car, *intending to find his birth mother* now that the obstacle he perceived as preventing it, his adoptive parents, was gone. Although the Prosecution claimed that Patrick had been angry because his adoptive parents refused to pay his Emergency Room bill for minor cuts and bruises, and then refused to accept his collect all, his defense attorney and psychoanalysts claimed "anguish over his adoption as a small child contributed to his insanity. "

Campbell was a special education student who spent much of his adolescence in state institutions. At age 15, he had been arrested in Darien, Connecticut, for indecent exposure and breach of the peace, both misdemeanors. He returned home at 17 and his adoptive parents were determined to have him finish high school. He graduated from a private school in Fairfield, but then was unable to hold a job, even at a Danbury fast food place, usually being fired or just no longer showing up.

His parents then told him *"Find a job and keep it, or join the service - the Army or Navy - or leave the house."* He then resided about 6 months with a family of a friend and spent the next year on the streets of Norwalk, spending nights in a homeless shelter. He was allowed to come home for visits, but the Campbells required that he call first and didn't give him a house key. Patrick was believed to be last living in a tent near a Danbury Mall as he was not wanted at the Campbells' home. Neighbors said he had long battled with his adoptive parents. He told media "About a year ago, I was going to kill my [adoptive] parents. I went into the house by breaking a window and climbed in. I was waiting for them to come home... but I fell asleep." When his parents came home and found him there, they threw him out of the house.

Betty Jean Lifton, psychologist, and herself an adoptee, theorized that a series of rejections by his adoptive parents and girlfriends caused his already "split self" to snap in fear of a second abandonment – the first being abandonment for adoption. Patrick was allowed to meet and talk with his biological mother for the first time after his court hearing. After their meeting, he commented *"If only I could have seen and talked with her earlier, none of this would have happened."*

He was sentenced to 45 years in prison; at time of this publication is age 51 and has served about 31 years.

(--Source: *"Adoption Called Key To Killing"* Detroit Free Press, 4-22-88; Betty Jean Lifton, *"The Journey of the Adopted Self"*; Nick Ravo, *"Drifter Charged in Bludgeoning of Parents,"* New York Times, 7-3-87; *"Son, 20, Confesses To Killing Parents,"* New York Times, Metro Archives, 8-15-87.)

PATRICK DEGELLEKE, 14

Born in Ohio in 1974, Patrick DeGelleke was with his biological mother for the first 3 years of his life. His mother had turned to prostitution to keep food on the table and was gone from the house for long periods.

He was adopted at age 6 by John and Judith DeGelleke. Unable to have children of their own, they started adopting in 1975 by adopting 9-year old twin girls, Robin and Renee. A year later, they adopted Patrick, 6, and his 3 biological brothers, Christopher, 9, Matthew, 10, and Phillip, 12, from foster homes in Ohio. The sudden creation of a family led to "ongoing strain" and the family began attending group counseling sessions at a nearby hospital.

In 1984, his adoptive parents died as result of the fire set by their adopted son, Patrick, then 14. Patrick was tried as an adult when he turned 15. Expert for the defense, David Kirschner, Phd, a Long Island clinical psychologist, testified that the trauma of adoption and a fear of abandonment may have produced a psychotic, insane **rage** in Patrick when he set the fire. One aspect of the defense case offered by Kirschner was the concept known as "Adopted Child Syndrome," unproven and unrecognized in psychiatric manuals, Kirschner said in an interview: "Patrick's **rage** was not so much directed at the DeGellekes," *"I believe he was really trying to destroy the adoption system which had upset his life."*

Judith DeGelleke died that day, but John DeGelleke survived for 10 days before he died from complications from his burns, according to a 1979 report presented at the trial.

Patrick was "a special problem," according to court testimony. He was a quiet, withdrawn child who could erupt into violent uncontrollable temper tantrums. He had few friends, and even his brothers seldom played with him. They often beat him up. When he was 8, he told a school psychologist *My mind is weird.* In school, he was disorganized, had concentration problems, and needed constant supervision. He would often stare blankly into space for hours at a time. He read "The Adventures of Huckleberry Finn" and dreamed of running away, hiding in the woods and *searching for his natural mother.*

As a teenager, his disciplinary problems grew worse, and included truancy, theft and general rebelliousness, witnesses testified. His adoptive parents filed a petition with Family Court, saying they could not control him and asking the court to intervene.

Patrick said he never intended for anyone to be hurt but wanted people to think he died in the fire so he could hop a train back to Ohio, find his mother, and live happily ever after. He had an **absence of feelings** about his adoptive parents who treated adoption with a sense of "denial."

Patrick served 9 years, was released from prison, and was last known to be living with one of his adoptive sisters.

(--Source: *"Violence in Adoption,"* a talk by Donald Humphrey, adoptee/attorney, 9-23-92 conference of The American Adoption Congress; and *"Expert Testifies Youth Killed Parents Because of Adopted Child Syndrome, New York Times,"* 2-18-88)

JORDAN MARIN-DOAN, 16

Jason Doan, 45, and Alan Marin, married the day that gay marriage was legalized in Indiana in 2014. In 2016, they adopted 3 children – an 11-month old, a 10-year old, and Jordan, 16.

Jordan admitted he poured fuel on the carpet of a stairwell in the house, and then, using a lighter, ignited the fire that killed one of his adoptive fathers, Jason Doan, on November 2, 2017. Doan's husband, Alan Marin, said they woke up to find fire blocking their exit and Doan helped Marin and their 2 adopted children escape through a window before Doan succumbed to the flames and smoke inhalation.

Alan Marin told police that Jordan had been threatening to "kill everyone in the house" and said he wanted to kill his adoptive parents "so he could get a cell next to his biological father who was in prison."

The boy had a troubled past; his birth dad was arrested in front of him and he thought it was his fault because he did something wrong,

Alan Marin said. They tried to get him the best possible therapy but they couldn't get the kind of service that he needed right away.

Yet, at the time of Jordan's arrest he said he "did not know why he started the fire."

(--Source: Katie Cox, "16-Year-Pleads Not Guilty to Arson, Murder, in Adoptive Father's Death," RTV-6, 11-8-17; Jared Gilmour, "He Burned His Adoptive Dad Alive, Hoping to Join His Biological Dad in Prison a Family Member Told Police," Miami Herald, 11-10-17)

MATTHEW DION, 39

Matthew Dion admitted to killing his elderly adoptive parents, Robert Dion, 71, and Constance Dion, 67, at their Manchester, New Hampshire home in March 2014.

He strangled them both with wire, **then set fire to their home 5 days later, causing an explosion.** He was captured about a month after the murders in Florida where he was living and working while on the run under aliases Cameron Rowell, Cam Buchard, and Jacob Smith. Prosecutors said Matthew "had been living a life of lies that was about to unravel before the killings... He wasn't working but told everyone that he was working. He had been stealing rare [collector] stamps from his adoptive father and taking them to Boston to sell And he was having some pain with medical issues and relationship issues and it all came to a head."

After arrest, Dion stated "**I didn't even feel the guilt of what I did to my parents,**" he said. "I felt the guilt about what if one of those (firefighters) got hurt." He was charged with one count of Arson and 2 counts of Second Degree Murder. He was sentenced to 60 years in prison.

(--Source: Marc Fortier, Katherine Underwood, "*U.S. Marshal: 'He Killed His Parents, What's To Say He Won't Kill Again?'*" NECN.com. 11-20-14; Hailey Winslow, Harrison Barrus, "*'Most Wanted' Held on No Bond, Requests Return to New Hampshire,*" News-4, JAX.com, 6-4-15; Amy Covena, "*In Taped Confession, Dion Shows Little Remorse for Killing Parents,*" WMUR-9 TV, WMUR9.com, 7-10-16)

JAMES RYAN FRAZIER, 20

James Frazier was born September 22, 1983, and immediately adopted. At age 20, he pled guilty to the stabbing deaths of his adoptive parents, Daniel Frazier, 53, his wife, Sally, 50, and their biological son, John Michael Frazier, 17, **and setting their house on fire to conceal the slayings.** The family had been stabbed more than 10 times each, and the family dog had been stabbed 17 times. Reportedly, James has **never shown remorse**."

He was sentenced to Life in prison for the Murder charges, Plus 99 Years for the Arson -- meaning he won't be eligible for parole for 100 years. When the former Baylor student and Eagle Scout was asked if his adoptive parents treated him differently because he was adopted, than his younger brother who was their biological son, he said no and that his family never mistreated him.

Authorities believed James wanted to inherit a substantial amount of money in his adoptive parents estate. His attorney argued that he might suffer from a psychological disorder that could render him incompetent for trial. Despite more than 2 hours of videotaped interrogation Frazier's motives remained a mystery.

At age 35, Frazier posted to a penpal page on JMail.com, as follows:

> "It took me 18 months in jail to come to terms with reality and grow up enough to accept responsibility for the mistake I made. It took several years to really heal and make some peace with most of my baggage, especially regret, shame, and the struggle with pride, forcing myself to allow myself to be imperfect and working from there, confronting one issue at a time. As I told someone recently, it was some time in 2010 that I was able to take a look at myself and see a grownup, less baggage, and more 'me' than ever. I never thought I'd post this kind of profile, but then I realized that that my shyness was due to embarrassment, asinine as that sounds, over my circumstances, which I ought not let withhold me from having what enjoyment in life I can... After many years I still don't 'fit in' here, nor do I want to, so there are some extremely lonesome times but also room in my life for new people..."

(--Source: "*Former Baylor Student Pleads Guilty to Killing Family*," MyPlainview.com, 5-24-04; Elvia Aguilar, "*Frazier Gets Life in Prison*, Baylor Lariat Archives, 8-23-04; JMail.com website, Rosharon, Texas)

MARJORIE CALDWELL HAGEN

In 1979, Marjorie Hagen was legally acquitted of smothering to death her adoptive mother and the beating death of a night nurse, which didn't mean that she hadn't killed her. In 1985, she was imprisoned **for setting fire to a house** for insurance money. In 1988, her second allegedly husband killed himself. Having previously killed Wally Hagen's first wife, Helen, in 1980. In 1992 at age 60, she is *suspected* of killing her third husband, Wally Hagen, 82, who had cancer and was given 2 months to live. **But she was *convicted* of setting a fire at a neighbor's home, one of a rash of fires** plaguing this small town.

(--Source: John Pacenti, *"She Seemed So Nice..."* Los Angeles Times, and AP, 11-29-92).

JOSHUA BRADLEY JENKINS, 15

On February 2, 1996, using a hammer, knife and axe, Joshua Jenkins killed 5 members of his adoptive family – both of his adoptive parents, both adoptive grandparents, and his adoptive sister, in a Las Vegas home. Somehow Josh kept his 10-year-old sister, Megan, from discovering the carnage. The slayings occurred after an argument with his adoptive parents.

He then cleaned the murder weapons, took a shower, changed clothes, set the place on fire and left.

Josh had always wanted to know about his birth parents but was never told. His adoptive parents said they had a letter from his mother *but refused to show it to him* because of their desire to replace his parents. He said he thought his "birth" parents had abandoned him. When placed at Vista del Mar for treatment, he felt his adoptive parents had also abandoned him. Four psychiatrists agreed that the boy suffered from chronic depression. A day before his 1997 trail, Josh changed his plea to Guilty which spared him the Death Penalty and was sentenced to 112 to 140 Years in Prison.

(--Source: *Las Vegas Review Journal*, 4-17-97)

JOHNNIE MICHAEL COX

Cox was convicted of killing his adoptive grandmother, Marie Sullens, 68; Margaret Brown, 34; and Billy Brown, 32, **who he bound, shot, stabbed and strangled, then set their home afire.**

On November 1, 1989, Cox went to Marie Sullens' apartment to kill her. He had chosen that date, All Saints Day, because he thought she would go to heaven if she died on that day. Sullens was married to Cox's grandfather. He later told police that he had killed Sullens because he suspected that she was trying to kill his grandfather.

When he arrived at her apartment, he found that Margaret and William Brown were there, too. Shortly after he arrived, Cox threatened William Brown with a .22 pistol and ordered him to bind Sullens and Margaret Brown with duct tape. Cox then tied up William and bound all three together at the neck. He first tried to sedate the three victims with sleeping medication. Because the drug took too long to take effect, he stabbed the victims and also attempted to shoot Margaret Brown.

Later, unhappy with the delayed effect of the stabbing, Cox attempted to strangle the three victims and then set fire to the house. All three individuals died as a result of stab wounds and injuries from the fire. Margaret Brown died *before* the fire as a result of fourteen stab wounds and strangulation. William Brown had wires around his neck and two stab wounds, but **died in the fire**. Sullens had six stab wounds, some penetrating her lungs, but also **died in the fire.**

Johnnie Cox was executed by lethal injection on February 16, 1999 in Arkansas for the 3 murders.

(--Source: *Death Penalty* website, prodeathpenalty.com/)

TIMOTHY STURGEL

Jerry Sturgel had 3 adopted children, and had previously been a foster father.   Timothy Sturgel shot his adoptive father to death **just before setting the house on fire.** When police finally made it into the house, they found two other victims: Sturgel's wife, Mary, 40, and Mary's daughter, Emily Hurst, 13.

When Timmy saw police, he raced around to the side of the house and slid inside the door as police surrounded the single-story ranch home. After a few minutes, he popped out the back door, pointed the weapon toward deputies and then quickly stepped back inside again. Moments later, the back door opened again; this time Timmy left behind the weapon and held his hands in the air. He surrendered. That's when police noticed the smoke.

Timmy reportedly "heard voices." Jerry Sturgel's patience with Timmy was wearing thin and he was about to put him out of the home. Timothy was charged with 3 counts of Murder.

 (--Source: *"Son Charged with Murder in Family Killings,"* Enquirer.com, 1-24

ANGEL PETERSON

Angel Peterson ended the abuse by her adopters when **she threw a firebomb through a window** while her adoptive slept, trapping and killing the couple who adopted her 8 years prior.

(--Source: *"Fatal Bombing Was Vengeance for Beatings,"* Detroit Free Press, 11-8-94)

MOSES KAMIN, 15

Moses Kamin was one of 3 children born to Rosa Smith, who had substance abuse and mental health issues. He was placed in a string of abusive foster homes, until age 6 when, in 2002, he was adopted in Oakland, California, by Susan Poff, who treated homeless patients at San Francisco's Housing and Urban Health Clinic, and Robert Kamin, a psychologist for the San Francisco jail system.

On January 26, 2012, Moses, who has a Black Belt in karate, strangled his adoptive mother after the two got into an argument over his suspension from school for smoking marijuana. He stashed her body and waited for his adoptive father to come home from work. Attacking him from behind, he put a plastic bag over his head and strangled him. He put their bodies in their vehicle; **investigators believe the teenager had tried unsuccessfully to set the car on fire.**

According to a psychological evaluation conducted the year Poff and Kamin adopted Moses, his behavioral issues included trouble sleeping, poor attention, aggression, cruelty to animals, and difficulty

relating to other children. He tended to engage in fantasy play with violent themes. The psychologist diagnosed Moses with Attention Deficit Disorder, Conduct Disorder, Reactive Attachment Disorder, and Borderline Intellectual Functioning.

He was charged "as an adult" with two counts of Murder in the strangling of his adoptive parents in California, a Death Penalty state. Officers found the bodies of Robert Kamin, 54, and Susan Poff, 50,

under blankets in the back of a PT Cruiser parked outside their house in Oakland's Lake Merritt district. Moses Kamin was arrested the next day after police said he gave a confession.

(--Source: Lauren Gonsalves, "*Helping Moses Kamin: Too Little Too Late?*, "The Chronicle of Social Change.org, 6-25-13; "*Moses Kamin, Oakland Teenager, Charged on Adoptive Parents' Murders,*" Huffington Post, San Francisco, 1-31-12; AP, 2-1-12; U-T San Diego News, and in 2012 an Alameda County Public Defender named Steckler, and his forensics expert, Tracy I. Carlis).

MATHEW LINDQUIST, 21

In the early morning hours on December 20, 2017, Mathew Lindquist waited for the "fake burglars" to show up at his adoptive parents' home in Griswold, Connecticut. He texted his would-be accomplices *"Don't pull up in any driveway, just go up the road and turn lights off."* Matthew, and the man who was running late, had a plan: The man was supposed to give him drugs in exchange for guns belonging to Matthew's adoptive father after his parents went to sleep. The "fake burglar" would tie Matthew to a chair to make the scene look authentic. And when police arrived, he would tell them that "two Black guys" were responsible for robbing his dad's gun safe. It was bolted to the ground, so Matthew's next text asked the man *"Yo bro... Can you pick the lock?"*

But nothing went according to plan.

By the end of the night, Matthew was dead, his adoptive parents were dead, his house was nearly burned to the ground, and the guns were missing from the safe. For months, Matthew's body was missing, too,

leading police to suspect Mathew Lindquist as a person of interest.

But on May 12, 2018, police interviewed Ruth Correa, 26, the woman who was in the car with her adoptive brother, Sergio Correa, the man who allegedly promised Matthew drugs in exchange for guns. She was arrested May 12, after telling police everything that happened after the pulled up on Matthew's street. In her unsealed arrest affidavit, she said Matthew hopped into the back seat of the Correa's car as it rolled up his street. He asked the man whether he brought the drugs. Allegedly Sergio told Matthew he wouldn't be getting any drugs until he got the guns. Matthew panicked, jumped out of the car and tried to run away. Sergio chased him with a machete and hit him on the back of his head, telling him he was "supposed to be his boy" but now he could not trust him and threatened to tie up Matthew for real, with zip ties and duct tape over his mouth. That's when Matthew started to "yell and freak out," Ruth said. She told police her brother began stabbing Matthew and she also stabbed him "about 10 times." They continued into the house, leaving Matthew in the woods knowing the basement door would be left open for them. But they apparently didn't anticipate running into Kenneth Lindquist who he started hitting with a baseball bat while Ruth fought off the family dog with a golf club.

According to Ruth's affidavit, when Janet Lindquist came from another room, aghast at the scene, Ruth grabbed her by the hand, pulled her into a bedroom telling her she *"didn't have to see this"* and urged Janet to just give them the keys to the gun safe and they would go. Janet asked why this was happening and Ruth told her it was *"because their adopted son had set them up."* But Sergio had already obtained the guns from the safe and while Ruth went looking around the house for things to steal, and made 3 trips to the car with the loot, she returned to find Sergio choking the woman to death when she tried to reach for the phone. Before they left, **Ruth poured a flammable liquid all over the basement and then her brother lit an exercise ball on fire.** It was still dark when they got into Matthew's car and drove away with all the stolen property in the trunk. By the time Connecticut State Police and the Griswold Fire department arrived at the Lindquist home – at about 5:45 AM according to court records – the house was engulfed in

flames - **about the same time, roughly 40 miles away, that police in Glastonbury, Connecticut, responded to a vehicle fire; the car was registered to Matthew Lindquist and it didn't take police long to realize the two fires were connected**. But Matthew was nowhere to be found. Not long after finding Matthew's car, authorities in Glastonbury found a car registered to Kenneth and Janet Lindquist abandoned in an apartment complex parking lot. His parents were pulled from the rubble. Matthews adoptive brother told police Kenneth said they had been having problems with Matthew because he was abusing illegal and prescribed narcotics again. A neighbor said that, despite the drug issues, everything seemed to be going better for Matthew – until he lost his job earlier that week. By December 28, the Connecticut State Police considered Matthew the main "person of interest" in the deaths of his adoptive parents that were ruled homicides and police were asking the public for help in locating him. The whole time, is body was lying in the woods 1,500 feet from his home. A dog walker found his remains there on May 5, almost 5 months after he was killed. Matthew had been stabbed 40 times.

Janet Lindquist had died of injuries to her head and smoke inhalations, which means she was still alive when her house was set on fire. Kenneth Lindquist died from his skull fractures and traumatic brain injuries; no smoke was found in his lungs indicating he was dead before he fire started.

92

Sergio Correa maintains he "had nothing to do with this" and was charged with 3 violations of his probation including drug possession, pending further charges. Police arrested Ruth Correa on May 12, charging her with Murder, First Degree Arson, Home Invasion, and First Degree Robbery. Announcing the breakthrough in the case in a news release the Connecticut State Police said "detectives anticipate additional arrests."

(--Source: Meagan Flynn, "*A Son Helped Plan a 'Fake Robbery' of His Father's Guns, Police Say; He and His Parents Ended Up Dead*," Washington Post, 5-30-18; Dave Altimari, Nicholas Rondinone, and David Owens, "*Brother of Hartford Woman Arrested In Griswold Triple Homicide Also A Suspect*," The Hartford Courant, 5-15-18)

JAMES MICHAEL MUNRO, 18

In his own handwritten biography, Munro stated that he *attempted* to murder his adopters while they slept, **by pouring gasoline on their bed, intending to light a fire,** but they awoke, thwarting his plan which he then claimed "was a joke." They then placed him in a mental hospital.

Being mentally challenged, and having had physical handicap as well, he felt he was an *embarrassment* to them and that his parents *"wished the had never adopted him."* But in 1981, at age 20, when Jim asked to move back home, his adoptive parents declined and he attempted suicide over the rejection.

(--Source: "James Munro and the Freeway Killers" by Lori Carangelo, citing sources, including news clippings and Munro's prison and adoption records)

JAMES M. SNELL, 17

On October 9, 2016, James Snell **started a fire in the basement of his New Concord home intending to kill his adoptive family**. After he started the fire, he went upstairs to sit in the living room, directly over the fire in the basement, with his adoptive parents and 3 adopted siblings. Snell's adoptive father smelled smoke and got everyone out of the house." Eight months later, James confessed what he had done to a counselor, explaining that he had planned to set the fire without an accelerant to avoid being caught but should have set the fire after everyone was asleep.

He was charged as an adult and ultimately pleaded guilty to Arson and 5 counts of Attempted Murder and was sentenced to 21.5 years in prison. Common Pleas Judge Mark Fleegle commented that James started killing animals when he was young and "when that stopped being fun" he moved on to trying to kill people. While in County Jail, Snell assaulted an inmate and pled guilty to Aggravated assault.

(--Source: Kate Snyder, Zanesville Times Recorder, 4-13-18)

MICHAEL PILATO, 15

Michael Pilato was charged with Second Degree Murder and Arson, **He admitted he poured gasoline throughout the interior of the Webster, New York, residence and set it on fire with the intention of causing deaths.**

Killed were Carmen Pilato, his 71-year old adoptive father, and his brothers Peter, 16, and Joshua, 12. His adoptive mother, Elaine Pilato, 59 and his 13-year old adoptive sister, Elizabeth, escaped, but with injuries. Investigators offered no clues for his actions. Police said they had been called to the residence several times in the past year to investigate "missing person situations" but declined to elaborate because the complaints involved minors. Carmen and Elaine Pilato adopted several children after their biological children were grown. A judge entered Michael's Not Guilty plea and ordered a mental evaluation before sending him to a juvenile lockup to be held without bail.

(--Source: *"Newport Teen Set Blaze That Killed Adoptive Father, Two Brothers, Cops Say," AP/Huffingtonpost.com*, 2-7-11)

CODEE WHEELER, 16

Codee Wheeler was charged as an adult with Homicide, Arson, Aggravated Assault and related offenses, **in the 3-21-07 fire that killed her adoptive father,** William Earl Wheeler, 57, a former township supervisor.

According to the criminal complaint, Codee Wheeler had been removed from the home by Indiana County Children and Youth Services in December 2006 after her grandmother called police complaining about the girl's father. Codee told authorities her father would walk around the house, and into the bathroom while she was showering, wearing only his underwear. During the CYS investigation, William Wheeler was not allowed to have contact with the girl. But she believed he was listening in on phone conversations she was having with her mom and was upset after her mother took all the money from her bank account, police said. **"I could just burn the house down!" Codee said**, according to her friend's account to police.

A bus driver and students at Blairsville Senior High School said they saw Codee on the sidewalk outside her home that morning, as black smoke billowed from the house, talking on a mobile telephone, and declined offers of assistance. Prosecuting Attorney Patrick Dougherty argued that Codee's actions after the fire -- calling her mother first and waving off people who asked if she needed help -- were proof that she intended to kill her father. But a jury of 7 men and 5 women acquitted Wheeler of all criminal counts related to the house fire that killed her adoptive father.

(--Source: *"Teen Charged in Arson That Killed Her Adoptive Father,"* Georgie.com)

ISAIAH R. SWEET, 17

Over Mother's Day weekend in 2012, Isaiah Sweet murdered his legal guardians/adoptive grandparents, Richard Sweet, 55, and Janet Sweet, 62, with an assault rifle, in their Manchester (Iowa) home. The grandparents called police about Isaiah 18 times from March 2011 to April 11, 2012, when he **attempted to start fires in their home** and for hitting Richard Sweet, threatening to beat them up and **burn down their house**, According to the police dispatcher, Janet Sweet didn't want Isaiah charged.

In 2012, he pled guilty to 2 counts of First Degree Murder and was sentenced in 2014 to Life Without Parole." But in 2016, the Iowa Supreme Court ruled that juveniles like Sweet who are convicted on Murder cannot be given Life sentences with no chance of parole, citing it a cruel and unusual punishment given a growing consensus among neuroscientists that teenagers' brains have not fully developed, making them more likely to be influenced by peer pressure or impulses.

Sweet was re-sentenced that year, to Life in Prison with Possibility of Parole, and is being held in adult prison at Iowa Sate Penitentiary in Fort Madison where he completed rehabilitative programming during his first 4 years of incarceration. But the Parole Board it was too soon to grant him parole.

 (--Source: Stephen Gruber-Miller, "*Parole Denied for Youth Who Killed Grandparents and Won Supreme Court Case,*" Des Moines Register, 6-21-18).

BIBLIOGRAPHY

Anderson, Robert, *Second Choice: Growing Up Adopted.* Badger Hill, 1993.

Austin, Linda Tollet, *Babies for Sale: The Tennessee Children's Home,* Greenwood Press, 1993

Benet, Mary K., *The Politics of Adoption.* The Free Press, 1976.

Bloom, Dr Lee, *Growing Up Behind Locked Doors.* Rolling Stone Magazine, 1986.

Borders, Anthony, *A Mother's 18-Year Search Ends.* The Press-Enterprise, 5-18-87.

Bowlby, John, *Illegitimacy and Deprivation.* World Health Organization, Maternal Care and Mental Health Monograph Series 4, 2nd ed. 115,149, 152; *Childhood Mourning and It's Implications for Psychiatry,* American Journal of Psychiatry, The Alfred Mayer Lecture, p.481-498, 1961

Brodzinsky, David, Marshal D. Schecter, *The Psychology of Adoption.* Oxford University Press, 1990; *Being Adopted: The Lifelong Search for Self.* Anchor, 1993.

Brodzinsky, David, Marshal D. Schecter, and Robin Marantz Hening. *Being Adopted: The Lifelong Search for Self*, Anchor, 1993.

Cadoret, Remi J., *Biologic Perspectives of Adoptee Adjustment, in The Psychology of Adoption* (Brodzinsky), Oxford University Press, 1990,

Carp, E, Wayne, *Jean Paton and the Struggle to Reform American Adoption,* University of Michigan Press, 2014.

Chan, N. and J.H. Hollinger, *Families by Law, An Adoption Reader.* New York University Press, 2004.

Chesler, Phyllis, *Sacred Bond*; and *Mothers On Trial*, 1986.

Coles, Gary, *The Invisible Men of Adoption*, BookPOD, 2011.

Crawford, Christina, *Mommie Dearest.* Berkeley Publishing, 1984.

D'Arcy, Claudia Corrigan, *National Council For Adoption: Mothers, Money, Marketing and Madness,* Musings of the Lame, 2007.

Diver, Alice, *A Law of Blood Ties: The Right to Access Genetic Ancestry.* Springer Verlag, 2013.

Diver, Alice, *A Law of Blood Ties: The Right to Access Generic*

Ancestry, Springer Verlag, 2013.

Donalds, Elizabeth S., *Voices of Adoptees: Stories and Experiences Within the Schools*, Dissertation, Antioch University-New England, 2012.

Dorner, Patricia Martinez, *Adoption Search: An Ethical Guide for Professional,*. Catholic Charities, 1977.

Eldridge, Sherrie, *Twenty Things Adopted Kids Wish Their Adoptive Parents Knew,* Delta, 2009.

Fessler, Ann, *The Girls Who Went Away,* Penguin Books, 2007

Fisher, Nancy L, MD, MPH, *Cultural and Ethnic Diversity: A Guide for Genetics Professionals,* John Hopkins University Press, 1966.

Flango, Victor E. and Carol R., *The Flow of Adoption Information From the States,* National Center for State Laws, 1998.

Goldstein, L.A.; A.J. Solnit, *Beyond the Best Interests of the Child.* Free Press, 1972.

Griffith, Reverend Keith C., *The Right to Know Who You Are,* Katherine Kimball Publisher, 2012.

Hood, G., *Adoption or Abduction?* Dan Rather Reports, AXS TV, 2012

Humphrey, Attorney Donald, *Violence in Adoption* - a talk given at the American Adoption Congress Conference, 9/23/1992.

Kirk, David H., *Shared Fate: A Theory of Adoption and Mental Health,* The Free Press of Glencoe, 1994.

Kirschner, David M., *Son of Sam and the Adopted Child Syndrome.* Adelphi Society for Psychoanalysis and Psychotherapy Newsletter, June 1978; *Adoption Forensics: The Connection Between Adoption and Murder,* Crime Magazine, 2007.

Lifton, Betty Jean, *Journey of the Adopted Self*, Basic Books, 1994. *How to Adoption System Lights a Fire*, Los Angeles Times, 3/1/1996, *Twice Born, Memoir of an Adopted Daughter.* Other Press, 2006, *Lost and Found.* University of Michigan Press, 2009.

Mason, Mary M., *Emotional Disturbance in Adopted Children,* Prager Publishing, 1988.

Paton, Jean, *The Adopted Break Silence*, Orphan Voyage, 1954.

Reagan, Michael, with Joe Hyams, *On the Outside Looking In*, Zebra, 1998.

Riben, Marsha, *Shedding Light on the Dark Side of Adoption,* Harlo

Press, 1988.

Robinson, Evelyn Burns, *Adoption and Loss: The Hidden Grief*, Clova Publications, 2005.

Samuels, Elizabeth, *How Adoption in America Grew Secret*, Washington Post, 2001.

Sawyer, Josh, *Death by Adoption*, Cicada, 1979.

Silverstein, Deborah, MSW, and S. Roscia, BSW, MSW, *Lifelong Issues in Adoption* (in *Working with Older Adoptees*, Coleman, Hornby, Baggis.) University of Southern Maine, 1998.

Solinger, Rickie, *How the Politics of Choice Shaped Adoption, Abortion and Welfare in the United States*, Hill and Wang, 2001; *Wake Up Little Susie: Single Pregnancy and Race Before Roe v. Wade*, Routledge, 2000.

Sorosky, Arthur D., Annette Baran, and Reuben Pannor, *The Adoption Triangle*, Triadoption Publication, 2008.

Taylor, Elizabeth, *Are You My Mother?* TIME Magazine, October 1989.

Verrier, Nancy, *Primal Wound: Understanding the Adopted Child*, Gateway Press, 1998.

Wellisch, E., *Children Without Genealogy – A Problem of Adoption*, Mental Health-13, 1952.

Wilson-Buterbaugh, Karen, *The Baby Scoop Era: Unwed Mother, Infant Adoption and Forced Surrender*, Amazon Books, 2017.

DIRECTORY OF RESOURCES

ADOPTION LAWS BY STATE
bastards.org/activism/access.htm

ADOPTIVE PARENTS FOR
OPEN RECORDS and AGAINST
ADOPTION
Facebook.com/Anti-
AdoptionAdopters

ALANON / ALATEEN
Al-Anon-Alateen.org
wso@al-anon.org

AMERICA'S PROMISE Mentors
900 Washington St., Ste 400
Alexandria, VA 22314
americaspromise.org
local@americaspromise.org
1-888-559-6884

AMERICAN ADOPTION
CONGRESS
americanadoptioncongress.org
(202) 483-3399

AMERICAN BAR
ASSOCIATION
Washington, DC 20005-1019
aba.net
(202) 662-1000

AMERICAN CIVIL LIBERTIES
UNION (ACLU)
125 Broad St, 18th Floor
1-215-567-7000
New York, NY 10004
(212) 549-2500 ; aclu.org

--Capital Punishment Project
aclu.org/capital-punishment

--Prisoners Rights Project
aclu/org/prisoners-rights

AMERICANS FOR OPEN
RECORDS (AmFOR)
LoriCarangelo.com/AmFOR

AMERICA'S PROMISE
ALLIANCE
1110 Vermont Ave, NW-Ste 900
Washington, DC 20005
americaspromise.org
(202) 657-0600

AMNESTY INTERNATIONAL
3 Penn Plaza
New York, NY 100001
amnestyusa.org
1-800-AMNESTY;
(212) 807-8400;

BARBARA SINATRA
CHILDREN'S CENTER
(for young victims of child abuse)
39000 Bob Hope Drive
Rancho Mirage, CA 92270
BarbaraSinatraChildrensCenter.org
(760) 340-2336

BASTARD NATION
PO Box 1469
Edmond, OK 73083-1469
bastards.org

BIG BROTHERS / BIG SISTERS
230 North 13th Street
Philadephia, PA 19107
bbs.org
(215) 567-7000

BRIDGE OF HOPE
311 National Road
Exton, PA 19341
bridgeofhopeinc.org
(866) 670-HOPE

CAL FARLEY'S BOYS RANCH
and GIRLS TOWN USA
PO Box 1890
Amarillo, TX 79174-0001
calfarley.org; info@calfarley.org
(800) 687-3722

CARLIS, Tracy I., PhD
Adoption/Death Penalty expert
Carlis Psychological Services Inc.
16430 Ventura Blvd Suite 203
Encino, Calif. 91436
www.drtracylcarlis.com
drcarlis@drtracylcarlis.com
(818)713-0508

CENTURION MINISTRIES
Freeing the Innocent Committee
32 Nausau St, 3rd Floor
Princeton, NJ
criminaljustice.org
(609) 921-0334

CHILD WELFARE
INFORMATION GATEWAY
(Federal government website)
childwelfare.gov

CHILDHELP USA
childhelpusa.org
1-800-4-A-CHILD, 24/7 Hotline
1-800-922-8212

CHILDREN OF THE NIGHT
1450 Sylvan Street
Van Nuys, CA 91411

Ilee@childrenofthenight.org
1-800-551-1300 – Hotline
1-818-908-4474

CONCERNED UNITED
BIRTHPARENTS (CUB)
CUBirthparents.org

CPS WATCH INC
PO Box 974
Branson, MO 65615-0974
cpswatch/com
1-888-CPS-WATCH – Hotline
(417) 339-9192 - office

DATE OF BIRTH SEARCH
DOBSearch.com

DEATH PENALTY
INFORMATION CENTER
1320 Eighteenth St NW
Washington, SC 20036
deathpenalty.org
(202) 293-6970

DELANCEY STREET
FOUNDATION
Model substance abuse/
ex-con program
600 Embarcadero
San Francisco, CA 94017
DelanceyStreetFoundation.org
(415) 957-9800

DONOR CONCEPTION
NETWORK Worldwide Registry
PO Bo 265
Sheffield, England S3 7yX
United Kingdom

dcnetwork.org
cgnetwork@appleonline.net

DONOR OFFSPRING/PARENT
REGISTRY (Totally free)
LoriCarangelo.com/donoroffspring

FAMILIES AGAINST
MANDATORY MINIMUMS
(FAMM)
1612 "K" Street NW-Ste 700
Washington, DC 20006
FAMM.org
(202) 822-6700

FATHER FLANAGAN'S BOYS
TOWN
13603 Flanagan Boulevard
Boys Town, NE 68010
boystown.org;
hotline@boystown.org
1-800-448-3000 – National
Hotline

GENESIS HOUSE
621 – 34th Avenue /PO Box 22910
Seattle, WA 98122
genesishouse.com
info@genesishouse.com
(206) 328-0881

HOMEBUILDERS PROGRAM,
34004 – 16th Ave South, Ste 200
Federal Way, WA 98003-8903
strengtheningfamilies.org
(253) 874-3630 – Seattle

(253) 297-1550 – Tacoma

HOMELESS SHELTER
DIRECTORY
homlessshelterdirectory.org

HOMES NOT JAILS
1-877-50-SQUAT

INNOCENCE PROJECT
Benjamin N.Cardozo School of Law
55 – 5th Ave, 11th Floor
New York City, New York 10003
innocenceproject.org
info@innocenceproject.org

INTERNATIONAL SOUNDEX
REUNION REGISTRY (ISRR)
isrr.org

MILITARY SEARCH
searchmil.com

ME TOO MOVEMENT
metoomvmt.org/
Facebook.com/MeTooMVMT/

NATIONAL ASSOCIATION OF
CHILD ADVOCATES (NACA)
1522 "K" St, NW
Washington, DC 20005-1202
childadvocacy.org
(202) 289-0777

NATIONAL ASSOCIATION OF
WORKFORCE BOARDS
(NAWB)
(Private Industry Councils)
1202 New York Ave NW, #350
Washington, DC 20005
nawb.org
(202) 289-2950

THE ULTIMATE SEARCH
BOOK– U.S & World editions

NATIONAL CENTER FOR
MISSING AND EXPLOITED
CHILDREN (NCMEC) –
missingkids.com/keyfacts
1-800-THE LOST ;
 (1-800-843-5678)

NATIONAL CRIMINAL
JUSTICE REFUGEE
INFORMATION SERVICE
(NCJRS)
PO Box 6000
Rockville, MD 20849-6000
ncjrs.org; askncjrs@ncjrs.org
1-800-851-3420

OFFICE OF REFUGEE
RESETTLEMENT (ORR) *to
locate separated immigrant kids
and families*
1-800-203-7001
information@ORRNCC.com
Administration for Children &
Families - Switzer Building,
330 C St SW, Rm 5123
Washington, DC 20201
Ph: 202-401-9246;
fax 202-401-1022

P.I. MALL – Private Investigation
Network – pimall.com

NATIONAL ORGANIZATION
FOR WOMEN (NOW)

733 – 15th St. NW – 2nd Floor
now@now.org

Washinton, DC 20002
(202) 628-8669
now.org; now.org/chapters

PRISONER LOCATOR, By State
ancestorhunt.com/prisonsearch
or Google a state's Dept. of
Corrections Inmate Locator
PRISONER LOCATOR-
California
inmatelocator.cdcr.ca.gov
SOCIAL SECURITY DEATH
INDEX
rootsweb.com
ancestry.com/search

SOS CHILDREN'S VILLAGES
Pompano Beach, Florida 33060
sos.bc.org (worldwide)
sosflorida.org (Florida project)
(954) 420-5043

UNITED NATIONS RIGHTS OF
THE CHILD PROJECT
UN Centre, Plais des Nations
CH-1211 Geneva 10
Switzerland
unicef.org/crc

WOMEN'S ALTERNATIVE
CENTER PROGRAM
225 S Chester Rd, #6
Swathmore, Pennsylvania 19081
womensassoc.org
(610) 543-5022

WORLDWIDE PHONE BOOKS
www.phonebooksoftheworld

ADDENDUM

FIRESETTING and the
IMPULSE CONTROL DISORDER of PYROMANIA

ADOPTEES' OUTCOMES

Fire Setting
and the Impulse-Control Disorder of Pyromania

R. Scott Johnson , M.D., J.D., LL.M., Elisabeth Netherton , M.D.R. Scott Johnson
Published Online: 19 Apr 2017 - https://doi.org/10.1176/appi.ajp-rj.2016.110707

Sections:

For some few individuals, fascination with fire veers from a healthy respect to an unhealthy obsession. In rare instances, susceptible individuals may suffer from a buildup of tension that can only be relieved by deliberate fire setting, and that cycle of behavior is believed to represent the crux of the mental disorder called Pyromania. Therefore, mere fires setting is not at all pathognomonic for Pyromania.

The term "pyromania" was first used in 1833 by Marc and was derived from the 19th-century term monomania, which described a type of insanity characterized by impulsive acts devoid of motive(1).

The DSM-5 defines pyromania as requiring the following criteria:
- Deliberate and purposeful fire setting on more than one occasion.
- Tension or affective arousal before the act.
- Fascination with, interest in, curiosity about, or attraction to fire and its situational contexts (e.g., paraphernalia, uses, consequences).
- Pleasure, gratification, or relief when setting fires or when witnessing or participating in their aftermath.
- The fire setting is not done for monetary gain, as an expression of sociopolitical ideology, to conceal criminal activity, to express anger or vengeance, to improve one's living circumstances, in response to a delusion or hallucination, or as a result of impaired judgment (e.g., major neurocognitive disorder, intellectual disability, substance intoxication).
- The fire setting is not better explained by conduct disorder, a manic episode, or antisocial personality disorder. (2, pp. 476–477)
-

Per the DSM-5, "individuals with this disorder are often regular 'watchers' at fires in their neighborhoods, may set off false alarms, and derive pleasure from institutions, equipment, and personnel associated with fire. They may spend time at the local fire department, set fires to be affiliated with the fire department, or even become firefighters" (2).

Historical Perspective: For over 150 years, a schism existed to some extent within U.S. psychiatry as to whether Pyromania even existed as a mental disorder. Some saw it solely as a form of either insanity or as a wholly criminal act, while others viewed Pyromania as a legitimate mental disorder worthy of diagnostic consideration (3). Ultimately, as psychiatry grappled with issues of personal accountability over the course of the latter half of the 20th century, the concept of pyromania as a legitimate mental disorder eventually won out (3), with exceptions for clearly criminal or psychotic behavior, as elucidated in the DSM-5 criteria above.

Research Findings

Epidemiology of Fire Setting and Pyromania

Fire setting is predominantly a male condition. In a landmark study by Lewis and Yarnell (4) of 1,145 fire setters, over two-thirds of the perpetrators were male. Intelligence may play a role in fire setting behavior. Roughly 70% of the adults in the aforementioned case series were below the range of normal intelligence. In a study by Grant and Kim of 21 individuals with pyromania, the mean age at onset was 18 years (SD=6). Eighty-six percent reported urges to set fires, and subjects reported setting a fire every 6 weeks (SD=4), on average. Forty-eight percent met criteria for an impulse-control disorder, and 62% had a comorbid mood disorder (5).

Prevalence of Pyromania

Pyromania is a rare disorder, and research with regard to it is infrequently conducted, generally involving small numbers of patients. With regard to its prevalence, in separate studies of 113 arsonists (6), 191 state hospital patients with a history of fire setting (7), and 27 female fire setters (8), none were diagnosed with pyromania (9). Similarly, in a Finnish study of 90 arson recidivists, only three (3.3%) met DSM-IV-TR criteria for pyromania (10). Nine other arson recidivists would have met pyromania criteria but did not because they were intoxicated with alcohol at the time of the fire setting, thus failing to meet criterion E. Additionally, in a 1967 U.S. study of 239 convicted arsonists using different DSM criteria, pyromania was found to be the motive in 23% of such cases (11). In 1967, the applicable DSM criteria did not preclude a diagnosis of pyromania for individuals who were under the effects of substance intoxication at the time of the fire setting.

Nosology of Pyromania

Pyromania's classification within the DSM has evolved over the years. It began as an obsessive-compulsive reaction in DSM-I. It was dropped in DSM-II. When it returned in DSM-III, it was an impulse-control disorder, a category that has now been rolled up into DSM-5's disruptive, impulse-control and conduct disorders.

Sexual Gratification

Cases of fires being lit for sexual gratification appear to be rare. Examination of 1,145 adult male fire setters found that 40 (3.5%) engaged in such behavior for sexual arousal (10). A subsequent study of 243 male fire setters revealed that only six persons (1.2%) did so (12).

Children and Adolescents

Fire setting has been extensively studied in children, where it is commonly comorbid with attention deficit hyperactivity disorder (13). Multiple factors have been found to contribute to the emergence of this behavior, including maltreatment (14) and family stress, with experimentation and boredom being common reasons given for the fire setting (13). There is little in the literature, however, specifically addressing pyromania. One case report did document the development of pyromania in a 9-year-old boy after escitalopram was started for separation anxiety and encopresis, which resolved with cessation of the escitalopram (15). Despite some early research suggesting a link between the Macdonald Triad of enuresis, cruelty to animals and fire setting (10), subsequent research found no relationship between enuresis and fire setting recidivism (16). Other discussions of treatment options in the literature focus primarily on children and adolescents and involve parenting training (17), as well as various forms of therapy and relaxation training (18).

In children and adolescents exhibiting fire setting behavior, the differential diagnosis should include conduct disorder, pyromania, and curiosity fire setting. Children who merely experiment with matches as a part of normal adolescent development should be considered curiosity fire setters instead of being diagnosed with conduct disorder, as they lack the intent to cause serious damage.

Tarasoff: Duty to Warn and Protect

Given fire setting's propensity for property damage and risk for loss of life, it should be noted that a history of fire setting in a patient may give rise to a Tarasoff duty to warn and/or protect on the part of psychiatry residents. Clearly this duty is jurisdiction-dependent, and residents should be familiar with the Tarasoff statutes or case law in the state in which they practice.

Imaging and Treatment

In at least one case report, imaging has revealed an abnormality that may have been related to the pyromania itself. Specifically, an 18-year-old male who met criteria for pyromania was found to have a left inferior frontal perfusion deficit on single-photon emission computed tomography imaging. Following 3 weeks of cognitive-behavioral therapy (CBT) and 1 week of topiramate (75 mg daily), the patient reported a complete remission in his urges to set fires (19). In another case report, a man with a diagnosis of pyromania, whose condition was so severe that he had been accused of setting an individual on fire, was successfully treated with olanzapine and valproic acid. He experienced a subsequent abatement of his fire setting behaviors (20). In other patients, treatments with selective serotonin reuptake inhibitors, antiepileptic medications, lithium, antiandrogens, or atypical antipsychotics have been proposed (1). Furthermore, CBT has displayed some promise (1).

Conclusions

Many misperceptions exist about pyromania, one being that the majority of fire setters suffer from pyromania. However, the limited research on this condition does not support that proposition. Fire setting is not at all pathognomonic for pyromania, as many fire setters engage in such behavior for reasons other than anxiety relief, such as a result of schizophrenia, manic episodes, and personality disorders. Thus, psychiatry residents should be aware that pyromania is an extremely rare disorder that must not be confused with fire setting motivated by a criminal motive or which occurs under the influence of a substance. Furthermore, for the vast majority of adolescent fire setters who often set fires out of boredom or experimentation, pyromania would not be the correct diagnosis due to the DSM requirement of a buildup of tension and subsequent relief provided by fire setting. Persons diagnosed with pyromania are predominantly male, with the mean age being 18 years old, and fires are typically set every 6 weeks. Approximately half of these individuals suffer from a comorbid impulse-control disorder.

Another misperception about pyromania is that the act of fire setting is engaged for sexual gratification. However, the data similarly fails to support that contention, with only 1.2% of fire setters in one study doing so for sexual arousal. Additionally, residents should be aware that the Macdonald triad of enuresis, cruelty to animals and fire setting, borne out in early studies has not held up in a later study with regard to the enuresis component and its link to fire setting recidivism. Lastly, the discussion of treatment options has largely been limited to case reports, given the rarity of the condition. This highlights the need for further research regarding this rare yet important psychiatric condition that, if left untreated, can result in considerable property damage and the loss of innocent life.

Key Points/Clinical Pearls

Pyromania is quite rare. In a study of 90 arson recidivists, only three met criteria for pyromania. Individuals with pyromania suffer from a buildup of tension that can only be released by deliberate fire setting.

Patients who set fires due to being antisocial, merely for entertainment, or while under the influence of a substance cannot meet criteria for pyromania.

Regarding treatment, selective serotonin reuptake inhibitors, topiramate, valproic acid, and olanzapine each have some support in the literature, depending on patient comorbidities.

Dr. Johnson is a fellow in forensic psychiatry at Harvard/Massachusetts General Hospital, Boston. Dr. Netherton is a fourth-year resident in the Department of Psychiatry, Baylor College of Medicine, Houston.

References

1. Burton PRS, McNiel DE, Binder RL: Firesetting, arson, pyromania, and the forensic mental health expert. J Am Acad Psychiatry Law 2012; 40:355–365 Google Scholar
2. American Psychiatric Association: Diagnostic and Statistical Manual of Mental Disorders, 5th ed. Washington, DC, American Psychiatric Publishing, 2013, pp 476–477 Crossref, Google Scholar
3. Geller JL, Erlen J, Pinkus RL: A historical appraisal of America's experience with "pyromania": a diagnosis in search of a disorder. Int J Law Psychiatry 1986; 9:201–229 Crossref, Google Scholar
4. Lewis NDC, Yarnell H: Pathological firesetting (pyromania). Nerv Ment Dis Monogr 1951; 82:8–26 Google Scholar
5. Grant JE, Kim SW: Clinical characteristics and psychiatric comorbidity of pyromania. J Clin Psychiat 2007; 68:1717–1722 Crossref, Google Scholar
6. Prins H, Tennent G, Trick K: Motives for arson (fire raising). Med Sci Law 1985; 25:275–278 Crossref, Google Scholar
7. Geller JL, Bertsch G: Fire-setting behavior in the histories of a state hospital population. Am J Psychiatry 1985; 142:464–468 Link, Google Scholar
8. Harmon RB, Rosner R, Wiederlight M: Women and arson: a demographic study. J Forensic Sci 1985; 30:467–477 Crossref, Google Scholar
9. Soltys SM: Pyromania and firesetting behaviors. Psychiat Ann 1992; 22:79–83 Crossref, Google Scholar
10. Lindberg N, Holi MM, Tani P, et al.: Looking for pyromania: characteristics of a consecutive sample of Finnish male criminals with histories of recidivist fire-setting between 1973 and 1993. BMC Psychiatry 2005; 5:47 Crossref, Google Scholar
11. Robbins E, Robbins L: Arson with special reference to pyromania. NY State Med J 1967; 67:795–798 Google Scholar
12. Rice ME, Harris G: Firesetters admitted to a maximum security psychiatric institution. J Interpers Viol 1991; 6:461–475 Crossref, Google Scholar
13. Lambie I, Ioane J, Randell I, et al.: Offending behaviours of child and adolescent firesetters over a 10-year follow-up. J Child Psychol Psychiatry 2013; 54:12 Crossref, Google Scholar
14. Root C, MacKay S, Henderson J, et al.: The link between maltreatment and juvenile firesetting: correlates and underlying mechanisms. Child Abuse Neglect 2008; 32:161–176 Crossref, Google Scholar
15. Ceylan MF, Durukan I, Turkbay T, et al.: Pyromania associated with escitalopram in a child. J Child Adol Psychop 2011; 21:381–382 Crossref, Google Scholar
16. Slavkin ML: Enuresis, firesetting, and cruelty to animals: does the ego triad show predictive validity? Adolescence 2001; 36:461–466 Google Scholar
17. Kolko DJ: Multicomponent parental treatment of firesetting in a six year old boy. J Behav Ther Exp Psychiatry 1983; 14:1349–1353 Crossref, Google Scholar
18. Kokes MR, Jenson WR: Comprehensive treatment of chronic fire setting in a severely disordered boy. J Behav Ther Exp Psychiatry 1985; 16:81–85 Crossref, Google Scholar
19. Grant JE: SPECT imaging and treatment of pyromania. J Clin Psychiat 2006; 67:6 Crossref, Google Scholar
20. Parks RW, Green RDJ, Girgis S, et al.: Response of pyromania to biological treatment in a homeless person. Neuropsychiat Dis Treat 2005; 1:277–280 Google Scholar

References

1. Burton PRS, McNiel DE, Binder RL: Firesetting, arson, pyromania, and the forensic mental health expert. J Am Acad Psychiatry Law2012; 40:355–365 Google Scholar

2. American Psychiatric Association: Diagnostic and Statistical Manual of Mental Disorders, 5th ed. Washington, DC, American Psychiatric Publishing, 2013, pp 476–477 Crossref, Google Scholar

3. Geller JL, Erlen J, Pinkus RL: A historical appraisal of America's experience with "pyromania": a diagnosis in search of a disorder. Int J Law Psychiatry1986; 9:201–229 Crossref, Google Scholar

4. Lewis NDC, Yarnell H: Pathological firesetting (pyromania). Nerv Ment Dis Monogr1951; 82:8–26 Google Scholar

5. Grant JE, Kim SW: Clinical characteristics and psychiatric comorbidity of pyromania. J Clin Psychiat2007; 68:1717–1722 Crossref, Google Scholar

6. Prins H, Tennent G, Trick K: Motives for arson (fire raising). Med Sci Law1985; 25:275–278 Crossref, Google Scholar

7. Geller JL, Bertsch G: Fire-setting behavior in the histories of a state hospital population. Am J Psychiatry1985; 142:464–468 Link, Google Scholar

8. Harmon RB, Rosner R, Wiederlight M: Women and arson: a demographic study. J Forensic Sci1985; 30:467–477 Crossref, Google Scholar

9. Soltys SM: Pyromania and firesetting behaviors. Psychiat Ann1992; 22:79–83 Crossref, Google Scholar

10. Lindberg N, Holi MM, Tani P, et al.: Looking for pyromania: characteristics of a consecutive sample of Finnish male criminals with histories of recidivist fire-setting between 1973 and 1993. BMC Psychiatry2005; 5:47 Crossref, Google Scholar

11. Robbins E, Robbins L: Arson with special reference to pyromania. NY State Med J1967; 67:795–798 Google Scholar

12. Rice ME, Harris G: Firesetters admitted to a maximum security psychiatric institution. J Interpers Viol1991; 6:461–475 Crossref, Google Scholar

13. Lambie I, Ioane J, Randell I, et al.: Offending behaviours of child and adolescent firesetters over a 10-year follow-up. J Child Psychol Psychiatry2013; 54:12 Crossref, Google Scholar

14. Root C, MacKay S, Henderson J, et al.: The link between maltreatment and juvenile firesetting: correlates and underlying mechanisms. Child Abuse Neglect2008; 32:161–176 Crossref, Google Scholar

15. Ceylan MF, Durukan I, Turkbay T, et al.: Pyromania associated with escitalopram in a child. J Child Adol Psychop2011; 21:381–382 Crossref, Google Scholar

16. Slavkin ML: Enuresis, firesetting, and cruelty to animals: does the ego triad show predictive validity?Adolescence2001; 36:461–466 Google Scholar

17. Kolko DJ: Multicomponent parental treatment of firesetting in a six year old boy. J Behav Ther Exp Psychiatry1983; 14:1349–1353 Crossref, Google Scholar

18. Kokes MR, Jenson WR: Comprehensive treatment of chronic fire setting in a severely disordered boy. J Behav Ther Exp Psychiatry1985; 16:81–85 Crossref, Google Scholar

19. Grant JE: SPECT imaging and treatment of pyromania. J Clin Psychiat2006; 67:6 Crossref, Google Scholar

20. Parks RW, Green RDJ, Girgis S, et al.: Response of pyromania to biological treatment in a homeless person. Neuropsychiat Dis Treat2005; 1:277–280 Google Scholar

ADOPTEES' OUTCOMES

"We must assume that, after an adoption placement,
no news is good news."
--Eunice Baker, former social worker
at The Children's Center, a foster-adoption agency,
Hamden, Connecticut

"Negative adoption-related statistics have been published as early as the 1950s (by Jean Paton, MA MSW, herself an adoptee) and since the 1980s "negative" stats have often been suppressed -- for example:

45% of all 602s (felonies committed by juveniles)
are committed by Adoptees
(Source: June Idler, Interstate Compact On Children,
Riverside County, California Juvenile Probation Department, 1988)

"Negative" adoption studies, articles and books since the late 1980s were often similarly "censored." In a **2014** report involving 400 Adoptive families in the United Kingdom:

80% of adoptions "broke down" due to violence by the Adoptee toward Adoptive Parents and siblings
(Source: 2014 report by the University of Bristol in the U.K.,
"from records research and from interviews with 400 Adoptive Parents.")

In the Bristol study, as in censored U.S. studies now available, where adoptions had "broken down," Adoptive Parents noted that moving the adoptee from the adoptive home had been triggered by a combination of challenging behaviors. The parents complained of inadequate support and "feeling blamed" for the child's difficulties. The Adoptive Parents in the study cited examples of having been "beaten, suddenly attacked, threatened, intimidated and controlled." Many Adoptive Parents said they "lived in fear." Child aggression and violence within the adoptive home raises important issues for post-adoption services and for children's services more generally. In recent years, an increasing number of stories aired by media have finally been calling attention to adoptees "negative outcomes" -- particularly *"Investigation Discovery (ID)"* TV which airs true murder stories 24/7, and *"Criminal Minds"* on CBS whcih often bases fictionalized stories on true murder cases in which the Un-Sub is profiled and turns out to be adopted. And a plethora of biographical books (such as *"Kondro"* and *"James Munro"*) as well as statiscal compilations, have documented an over-representation of adoptees who are serial killers, mass murderers, and parent killers (as in *"Chosen Children (2002 through 2019 editions),"* *"RAGE! How An Adoption Ignites a Fire,"* and the soon to be released *"No Remorse: 400 Adopted Killers"*) aimed explaining the reasons for the phenomenon, toward reform. The following statistics are excerpted from *"The Adoption and Donor Conception Factbook"* (2018):

CRIMINAL ISSUES –
GOVERNMENT UNDER-REPORTING vs. ADOPTEES' EXPERIENCE

"All adoptees are *at risk* of anti-social, acting out behaviors due their emotional and psychological pain from loss of their biological reality—behaviors that may escalate to petty crimes or violent felony crimes." (David Kirschner, PhD; and Attorney Donald Humprey, himself an adoptee in *"Violence in Adoption."*)

In 2013 - the **U.S. Government** "Adoption and Foster Care Analysis and Reporting System" (AFCARS) reported
9% of Adopted children vs. 4% of all children
are diagnosed with Depression (Age 2+);
26% of Adopted children vs. 10% of all children
are diagnosed with ADD/ADHD (Age 6+);
15% of Adopted children vs. 10% of all children

are diagnosed with behavior conduct problems (Age 2+);
14% of Adopted children vs. 9% of all children
are have problems social behaviors (Age 6+);
88% of Adopted children (vs. 94% of all children)
exhibit *"positive* social behaviors"

From 1986 through 2013, **private practitioners** reported:

**60-85% of teens at Coldwater Canyon Center
for Personal Development psychiatric facility were Adoptees;
most were referrals from Juvenile Probation Department.**
(Source: Dr. Lee Bloom, Former Unit Director, Coldwater Canyon Hospital, Hollywood, California,
reported in *"Growing Up Behind Locked Doors,"* Rolling   Stone magazine, 11-20-86)

**40% of psychiatric internees surveyed were Adoptees;
adopted children have a higher rate of emotional and psychological problems than the
general population of youngsters.**"
(Source: Dr. Phyllis Chesler, in *"Mothers On Trial,"* quoting Dr. William Murdoch, child psychiatrist at
Loma Linda University School of Medicine and Director of Charter Hospital-Redlands Child In-Patient
Unit)

70% of internees at Monroe Washington psychiatric facility were Adoptees.
(Source: Monroe facility counselor, and Washington Adoptee Rights Movement member, at a 1988
conference of the American Adoption Congress)

**20-35% of internees at several hundred private psychiatric hospitals in 13 regions were Adoptees –
This is 17 times the norm.**
(Source: Betty Jean Lifton, quoting from a report by an Illinois doctor at the 1988 conference of the
American Adoption Congress; and cited by Pannor; BIRCO Publishing; Lawrence)

28% of adolescents in drug rehabilitation and in substance abuse treatment ` programs are adopted.
(Source: Center for Adoptive Families)

**5-15% of the patient load in mental clinics is the average reported figure for Adoptees under
psychiatric care,** while government estimated that only 2% of the U.S. population were Adoptees. It was
theorized that a child's ignorance of his pre-adoption past causes **"genealogical bewilderment"** and so the
Adoptee is prone to dysfunction;

**12% of adolescents in private therapy were Adoptees;
20-30% of adolescents and children in psychiatric in-patient units were Adoptees.**
(Source: Lincoln Caplan, in *"An Open Adoption,"* as cited in Bottom Line, 9-15-90)

**"Adopted children are disproportionately represented with learning disabilities and organic brain
syndrome."** (Source: Schecter,*"Genetic Behaviors"*).

**"Adoptees are more likely to have difficulties with drug and alcohol abuse, as well as eating
disorders, attention deficit disorder, infertility, untimely pregnancies and suicide"**
(Source: Young, Bohman, Mitchell, Ostroff, Ansfield, Lifton, Schecter).

"Adoptees are more likely to choose alternate lifestyles." (Ansfield/ Lifton)

**"Alarmingly high numbers of Adoptees are sent to disciplinary schools *or are locked out of their
adoptive homes. "*** (Source: Anderson, Carlson).

"Adoption is a psychological burden to the Adoptee, relative to the separation of the child from the

mother." (Source: Arthur D. Sorosky, Annette Baran, Reuben Pannor in *"The Adoption Triangle: The Effects of Sealed Records on Adoptees, Birthparents and Adoptive Parents,"* Triadoption, 2008).

"Adopted children are more likely than their non-adopted peers to have Attention Disorders, anxiety and depression." (Source: Dale Gwilliam, co-founder of Adoption Media LLC, in *"Adoption USA Chartbook"*)

In 2004 - a comparative study was conducted in Illinois which identified the percentages of school-related issues present in children raised by their biological families and in different types of adoptive families (domestic infant, intercountry, and child welfare). In that study, adopted children had more unmet emotional needs, required more special education services, received more teacher complaints about their behaviors, and were more likely to be on a medication for their behaviors. (Source: Howard, Smith and Ryan, 2004)

PSYCHOLOGICAL ISSUES

Adoptees have been found to be at risk for psychological problems as result of being adopted.
The psychology practitioner's guidebook, *"Clinical Practice of Adoption,"* by Robin C. Winkler, Dirck Brown, Margaret Van Keppel, Amy Blanchard (Pergamon Press) estimates:
- **"1 in 14 persons are personally affected by adoption"** -
  a huge departure from the "58%" and "1 in 6 touched by adoption" statistics.

1953 - Jean Paton, MA, MSW, a clinical social worker and an Adoptee, conducted the earliest studies on how sealed records adoption affected Adoptees, which resulted in her book, *"The Adopted Break Silence."* Paton recognized the Adoptee's unresolved pain from being denied their true identity and pre-adoption reality and that the only way to heal that pain was through searching for and finding the truth of one's origins.

In *"The Boy Who Was Raised as A Dog,"* author Bruce D. Perry, MD, PhD, suggests: "Ultimately, what determines how children survive trauma, physically and emotionally or psychologically, is whether the people around them -- particularly the adults they should be able to trust and rely upon -- stand by them with love, support and encouragement." However, this theory doesn't take into account each child's individual threshold of resilience and the cumulative effect of multiple burdens -- that is, problems added to the problem of being taken from his biological parents who should "stand by" him and the problem of being adopted. Adoptive Parents who are misled to believe that "with love" all will be well, often find themselves confronted with damaged children who cannot be "fixed."

1975 - Remi Cadoret, MD, PhD began a rare longitudinal study to determine whether or not substance abuse and anti-social behaviors identified in Adoptees are inherited from their biological parents. Cadoret had graduated from Yale University School of Medicine but specialized in Psychiatry. His longitudinal study assessed 4 cohorts of Adoptees with case control, and was conducted as result of his single-handedly lobbying the Iowa Legislature to allow him to access to ***tens of thousands of confidential adoption records.*** This enabled him to identify Adoptees whose biological parents reportedly manifested extremely high levels of anti-social and substance abuse behaviors. He then matched the Adoptees with control Adoptees that had no biological link for substance abuse or anti-social behavior. resulting in the demonstration of the profound *influence of the environment on moderating effects of genetic factors* and by delineating developmental pathways through which substance use and anti-social behavior form, which produced an appreciation for the adoption paradigm in the understanding of behavioral illness. **Called *"The Iowa Adoption Studies,"* Cadoret's work, in some venues, dispelled the notion of attributing Adoptees' negative outcomes as necessarily inherited from the biological mother.** Yet the "bad seed" notion persists today, particularly by lobbyists explaining away Adoptees' "bad outcomes" by blaming their genes while seeking funding to increase adoptions which they portray as "all good."

1979 - Bouchard Twin Studies - Thomas J. Bouchard, professor of psychology and director of the Minnesota Center for Twin and Adoption Research, University of Minnesota, began the first longitudinal studies on twins raised apart when he came across twins (Jim Springer and Jim Lewis) who had been separated since birth and were reunited at age 39.

- Each of the twins, Bouchard later wrote, married women named Linda, divorced and
- both married the second time to women named Betty.
- One named his son James Allan,
- the other named his son James Alan., and
- both named their pet dogs Toy.
- Both twins had some Law Enforcement training
- Both had been a part-time Deputy   Sheriff in Ohio.
- Each did poorly in Spelling
- Each did well and Math
- Each did Carpentry, Mechanical Drawing and Block Lettering
- Each vacationed within the same
- Both twins began suffering tension headaches at age 19
- both were 6 feet, 180 pounds and had gained 10 pounds at the same time

By odd coincidence, both twins also had an adoptive brother named Larry. Bouchard assembled a team and applied for a grant to The Pioneer Fund in 1981, stating "Our findings continue to suggest a very strong genetic influence on almost all medical and psychological traits." This work became known as the Minnesota Study of Identical Twins Reared Apart (MISTRA),better known as *"The Minnesota Twins Project"* and more commonly referred to as *"the Bouchard Twin Studies."* The project evolved eventually included 400 sets of twins raised apart. TIME, U.S. News and Work Report, the New York Times and various TV programs reported on Bouchard's conclusions that "shyness, political conservatism, dedication to hard work, orderliness, intimacy, extroversion, conformity, and a host of other social traits are largely inheritable. Bouchard is the author of more than 170 publications (Source: Wikipedia)

While Bouchard was studying *similarities* between twins adopted apart, others were comparing the *differences* between Adoptees and the non-adopted population, particularly psychological differences. "Attachment Disorder," first advanced in the 1960s, was deemed applicable to a "sub-set of Adoptees," who also exhibit anti-social *"Adopted Child Syndrome"* (ACS) behaviors, which, although not endorsed by the American Psychiatric Association,. has been a theory supported by many famed psychologists (Kirschner, Sorosky, Schecter, Carlson, Simmons, Work, Goodman, Silverstein, Mandell, Menlove, Simon, Senturia, Offord, Aponti, Cross and others. (See Bibliography).

1978 - David Kirschner, PhD, studied *"Dissociative Disorder"* and its underlying *"Adopted Child Syndrome,"* and revealed the complexities of Adoptees' dual identities and secret pasts.

1988 - "Adopted Child Syndrome" was successfully used as a defense in the case of Patrick DeGelleke, 14, who was tried as an adult for the murder of his Adoptive Parents. Kirschner identified the syndrome as contributing to Patrick's psychotic rage when he killed his Adoptive Parents and set fire to their home. The *New York Times* account of the crime explained that DeGelleke's shocking act was, to him, the only way to remove what he perceived to be the barrier preventing him from finding his natural parents: his Adoptive Parents.

Betty Jean Lifton, psychologist, herself an Adoptee, and reform activist/writer, referred to these same Adoptee behaviors as *"Adoption Disease...which can lie dormant most of one's life...but it can stir malignancy in some Adoptees most of heir lives."*

David Cooke, a psychiatrist, *said "Adopted Child Syndrome is simply a new name for a phenomenon that has been observed since the 1950s"* ...as Jean Paton observed in the 1950s.

1988 - Dr. Berry Brazelton referred to *Adopted Child Syndrome* as "malarkey" in the press, and the psychiatric community would not accept the Adopted Child Syndrome theory. Perhaps pressured by a "politically correct" group who spent 24/7 on alt.adoption chat site discrediting negative adoption issues, Kirschner was careful to quantify Adopted Child Syndrome, stating it *"does not apply to the vast majority of adopted children* *who turn out as normal as anyone else"* -- and that *"only 10-15% of Adoptees display problems"* (methodology unknown). It seemed that, for a time, *"Adopted Child Syndrome"* was "out."

1989 - Christiane Capron and Michel Duyme (Paris, France) noted a shortcoming in adoption studies and set out to correct it. Previously, researchers seeking to understand the impact of nature and nurture on I.Q, consistent with the proposition that intelligence is mainly inherited, have almost always found that adopted youngsters more closely resemble their biological parents rather than their Adoptive Parents. Changing a child's life circumstances won't alter the hard facts of nature. But since poor families rarely adopt, those investigations have had to focus only on youngsters placed in well-to-do homes. Because most adopted children come from" poor" homes, almost nothing is known about adopted youngsters whose biological parents are "well-off." So Capron and Duyme presented a full cross-fostering study dealing with IQ, and found that children **adopted** by high-SES parents score higher than children adopted by low-SES parents; children **born** to high-SES parents score higher than children born to low-SES parents; and that there is no evidence for an interaction between these two factors on children's IQ.

1990 - Studies suggested that adopted children are at risk of more than a 10 to 1 chance for psychological maldevelopment when compared to children raised with their biological parents (Source: Anthony, 1990).

2007 - Five years after *"Chosen Children"* was published, Kirschner's "The Connection Between Adoption and Murder" was published on 9-17-07. Thereafter, Kirschner again revised is position, by writing "I believe that *most* **Adoptees** have the same emotional vulnerabilities that are seen in dramatic form in the Adopted Child Syndrome, and that *all Adoptees* **are at risk.**" Still later, he is careful to qualify that by claiming **only a "sub-set" of "a spectrum" of Adoptees** have Adopted Child Syndrome behaviors, but he does not define the spectrum in which the subset occurs, and so it may mean **"the entire spectrum of Adoptees,"** with extremes of acquiescence at one end of the spectrum, and of rebellion at the other end, in response to adoption's impositions. In other words, all Adoptees are at risk. *"Adopted Child Syndrome"* was again "in."

David M. Brodzinsky, PhD (Professor Emeritus, Clinical Psychology, Rutgers University; Research and Project Director, Evan B. Donaldson Adoption Institute) conducted one of the nation's largest studies of adopted children at Rutgers, which recognized that **adoption itself is a psychological burden to the Adoptee** and that their problems and symptoms often fall into the "Adopted Child Syndrome" pattern. Adoptees seem to have trouble trusting others and forming close relationships. Often they feel they don't belong, or are unloved and unwanted. With excessive fear of abandonment, they are constantly "testing limits" and seeking approval, affection, and acceptance. They experience a severe identity crisis in adolescence around whether they feel they are a full member of the adoptive family or just being loyal to their "rescuers." Finding their biological parents, or being found by them, can stress all parties, no matter the depth of, or lack of, a resulting relationship. Where Adoptive Parents have a "shape up or ship out" mentality, adolescent Adoptees are more likely to "act out." Though professionals agree that Adoptees should have access to their origins, politics thwart good sense.

ADOPTION DISSOLUTIONS DUE TO VIOLENCE

In the U.S., as early as **1998**, a study that examined the behavior problems of children receiving services through an "adoption preservation program for legally adopted children at risk of placement or dissolution," two measures of behavior problems were used:

- a behavior problem rating scale, available on 368 children, and
- the Child Behavior Checklist (CBC), available on 201 children.

Variables associated with **severity** of behavior problems include

- attachment problems,
- age at placement,
- experienced multiple types of abuse and neglect,
- a history of sexual abuse, and
- experienced a recent loss in the family.

The findings support the need for services for children and families beyond the finalization of adoption."
(Source: "An Analysis of Child Behavior Problems in Adoptions in Difficulty," S.L. Smith, J.A. Howard, A.D. Monroe, in the Journal of Social Services Research, 24(1/2), 6-84, 1998)

Post Traumatic Stress Disorder (PTSD) was first introduced into psychiatry in 1980, it was at first seen as a "rare" condition affecting only a minority of soldiers as result of combat experiences. But PTSD began being described in rape survivors, victims of natural disasters, and in people who had witnessed life-threatening accidents and injuries. Child psychology had not yet embraced neuroscience until the 1990s ("the decade of the brain") and there was active opposition by many psychiatrists and psychologists to taking **a biological perspective on human behavior.** Such an approach was "dehumanizing" and suggested that everything was caused by genes (or the mother, as Freud had claimed). Even today, many adoption advocates automatically suspect **pre-adoption experiences** where such history is usually unknown due to sealed records, without also considering **post-adoption experiences,** nor how the fact of **the adoptive status itself** resonates in the minds of adopted children and adults.

ADOPTEES WHO ARE FIRESETTERS

13% of 69 firesetters were adopted,
compared to a control group of non-firesetters,
3% of whom were not adopted,
(Source: Dr Wayne S Wooden and Dr. Martha Lee Berkey.
"Study of "Youthful Firesetters in the San Bernardino County, California Juvenile Justice System")

ADOPTEES WHO ARE SEX OFFENDERS
(according to State Department of Corrections-DOC websites, newstories, and/or their letters to AmFOR and their stories detailed in *"Chosen Children"* which details their adoptions):

ALEXANDER, Gerald "Ajax," 42 (Source: *Detroit News*, Michigan, 4-8-99)
BALL, Michael W., 15 (Source: Washington DOC; and Letters to AmFOR)
CAMPBELL, Frank Jayson, aka Hawk Rhal (Source: Maine DOC; and Letters to AmFOR)
GRAY, Steve (Source: Colorado DOC; and Letters to AmFOR)
HALE, Daniel Edward (Source: Ohio DOC; and Letters to AmFOR)
MITCHELL, Emanial (Source: Georgia DOC; and Letters to AmFOR)
PRINKEY, Robert Lee (Source: Pennsylvania DOC; and Letters to AmFOR)
REINAN, Tommy Lewis (Source: DOC; and Letters to AmFOR)
RIDER, Christopher Scott (Source: California DOC Public Record and Letters to AmFOR)
STROHMEYER, Jeremy, 18 (Source: *Los Angeles Times*, 7-19-98)
TIBBS, Chico Matthew (Source: Colorado DOC; and Letters to AmFOR)
WILLIAMS, Duane Harold (Source: Iowa DOC; and Letters to AmFOR)

Where adoptions had "broken down." Adoptive Parents noted that removal from their home had been triggered by a combination of the child's challenging behaviors, inadequate support, and "feeling blamed" for the child's difficulties. Adoptive Parents cited examples of being suddenly attacked or beaten by the children, and/or threatened, intimidated and controlled. Some had been prevented from leaving their homes and had their support networks undermined. Many Adoptive Parents said they "lived in fear." Child aggression and violence within the adoptive home raised important issues for pot-adoption services and for children's services more generally.
(Source: *"Local Authorities Underestimate Adoption Breakdowns, Study Suggests,"* Neil Puffet, "Children & Young People Now," 4-10-14)

OVER-MEDICATING ADOPTEES

David Kirschner, PhD, is quoted in the press as citing HMOs' tendency for limiting treatment of very young Adoptees misdiagnosed with Attention Deficit Hyperactive Disorder (ADHD) to mind altering drugs instead of therapy. Dexedrine, Cylert and the most widely prescribed Ritalin and Mellaril, are routinely administered to youngsters who are "acting out" in response to their inability to "attach" to their Adoptive Parents. They miss their families and the feeling of connectedness. Drugs cannot cure such pain. Why would HMOs approve central nervous system stimulants (CNS) over psychotherapy—drugs that are believed to have played a role in Adoptee Jeremy Strohmeyer's rape murder of 7-year old Sherrice Iverson in a Nevada casino restroom? According to Kirschner, the for-profit managed care corporations are opting for the less expensive drug therapy over psychotherapy. The drug industry is certainly not complaining and has also rebutted claims that drugs prescribed to children for disorders such as "hyperactivity" or depression, are likely to cause fatal heart attacks as in 7 unexplained deaths recorded in the late 1990s of children taking such drugs.

In 1998, Bennett Leventhal, a child psychiatrist at the University of Chicago, estimated that "6 to 10 of all children have ADHD but only 2 of the 6 were being treated for it." He further claimed that fears about overuse of drugs like Ritalin "are *unfounded.*" (Source: Arabia Living at Arabia.com,11-10-98).

Contrary to Leventhal's statement, Adoptees who are the subject of this writer's "true crime" books, including many of the hundreds of Adoptees in "*Adopted Killers,*" were given prescription drugs, including Ritalin and Mellaril, at an early age. And in many cases of Adoptees who have killed, they had been legally prescribed drugs or had taken street drugs just prior to their crime. The long term or permanent chemical changes in children's brains from mind altering, psychotropic drugs is still being studied, while the number of prescriptions for stimulants such as Ritalin and Dexedrine to treat ADHD, particularly in young children, has increased dramatically during the past 10 years. Over-and under-identification is a problem. There's no way to make an adequate medical or psychological assessment in a 7-minute visit, so what we have is a situation where teachers complain and physicians write a prescription. It takes the kind of time and effort that most physicians don't have and most insurers won't pay for." (Source: Daniel Kessler, MD, Director, Developmental and Behavioral Pediatrics, St. Joseph's Hospital and Medical Center, Phoenix, Arizona, in American Medical News, 11-20-00).

Novartis, the company that manufactures **Ritalin**, the American Psychiatric Association, and a patient advocacy group called CHADD-(Children and Adults with Attention-Deficit/Hyperactivity Disorder), were sued by several hundred parents charging that these groups conspired to over-promote diagnosis of ADHD to boost drug sales. DEA has classified **Ritalin** in the same category as Morphine, Opium, and Cocaine. Littleton, Colorado was the most notorious for doling out Ritalin to kids, particularly in wealthy suburbs as well as in public supported foster care. The long term effects are still being debated in the wake of the Columbine High School shootings in Littleton. Adoptees who became addicted to street drugs and those who killed were prescribed Ritalin (Methylphenidate), Mellaril (Thioridazine), and other mood altering drugs which led to their addictions and helped trigger violence against themselves and others. Not all traumatized children become suicidal or violent, and there are no simple answers to explain why some Adoptees kill. But often the side effects of prescribed drugs are overlooked. (Source: "*Reclaiming Our Children: A Healing Solution for a Nation In Crisis,*" Perseus, 2000)

Peter R. Breggin, MD, a private practitioner in Bethesda, Maryland, presents strong evidence that psychiatric drugs commonly *cause* psychoses and aggression in children, and that they probably contributed to individual cases of school violence. In his best selling "*Talking Back to Prozac*" and "*Talking Back to Ritalin*" he makes specific recommendations for improving family and school life based on sound psychological and ethical principles. But what if the family is a *shadow family*—a prohibition to the child under the unsound psychology and unethical practice perpetuated by closed adoption? What if the child does not accept his Adoptive Parents as "family?" No drug treatment or "attachment therapy" can change that, only compound the problem.

MEDICAL ISSUES

Adopted children may have undiagnosed/unknown or undisclosed/known medical, emotional or psychological conditions *pre-adoption*, or develop such conditions *post-adoption*.

Boruch Fishman, MD, PhD, solicited Adoptee responses to his survey that asked about "*ways in which physicians talk to Adoptees about their family history.*" He added an open text box to allow additional comments. The Adoptees' comments indicated there persisted not only a lack of interest, or even understanding, by primary physicians regarding *why* Adoptees have no medical history, but also an outright refusal to assist Adoptees in obtaining such medical history. (<u>Source:</u> on Adoption.com's "Adoption Forum," 7-4-08.)

Most state laws, and the Hague Convention, now require agencies to disclose "reasonably available" records. But it can be unclear, especially in international adoptions, how diligent agencies are expected to be in obtaining such information.

Adoptive Parents involved in closed *domestic* adoptions typically reported **that they avoided reporting Adoptees' minor to major medical or psychiatric problems discovered post-adoption, for fear of being perceived as incompetent to parent, or as being the cause of the problem,** while others preferred to consult their private physicians and therapists for fear that the child who the Adoptive Parents had waited for may be rendered *"unadoptable."* When the situation becomes more than the Adoptive Parents can handle any longer, these children may suffer emotional and physical abuse. In more recent adoptions of children who had first been neglected in *foreign* orphanages and have undisclosed problems, some Adoptive Parents have attempted to return the child to the agency or system.

The relative importance of "nature" (i.e., genetic inheritance) versus "nurture" (i.e., the rearing environment) in human behavior was first debated at the beginning of this century. The tort of "wrongful adoption" has been successfully litigated by Adoptive Parents who collected large damage awards by claiming that agencies *intentionally withheld* known information about the Adoptees pre-adoption medical conditions, physical or sexual abuse, mental health issues, or other pertinent family background. Before such wins in court, collection of pre-adoption medical information was "hit or miss", rather than mandatory practice as the 1980 Draft Model Adoption Act mandated and has only become codified in law and on a state-by-state basis in recent years.

While government (ObamaCare) and private insurers aggressively promote preventative health services, Adoptees' deaths at an early age can often be attributed to their lack of true family medical history still sealed in adoption records despite that there are more than 4500 known *inheritable* illnesses and disorders. Although, today, most states mandate provision of "non-identifying" information when requested by *adult Adoptees* from files that are 18, 21 or more years old, if they even still exist, most states have no practical scheme for communicating *updated* medical information from biological parents to Adoptees or Adoptive Parents, post-adoption. Older adoption files, may have contained extensive, scant, or no pre-adoption medical information on the child and on the child's biological relatives and caseworkers who have no medical education have often "summarized" or "excerpted" medical histories according to their own interpretation, at their discretion as to what will be disclosed.

Freundlich and Peterson's "recommendations for practice" includes a provision for "disclaimers" stating that "the agency can disclose only known health and other background information." Again, this seems to promote "agency's best interests" in waiving liability, rather than to compel any effort to solicit needed medical information in the child's best interests.

Americans For Open Records (AmFOR) documented many cases of state court judges refusing to open a "sealed" record and agencies refusing to disclose from "confidential" adoption files, even in life-and-death. (See *"Chronology on the Fight for Adoptees' Access to Medical Information"* and also: *"Adoption Uncensored: A 30-Year Collection of Selected Letters to AmFOR, 1977-2008, from Legislators, Agencies, Attorneys, Organizations, and Others on Adoption Issues"* at http://LoriCarangelo.com/uncensored)

The epitome of such hypocrisy may be exemplified in the website *"Adoption Medical News"* at http://adoptionmedicalnews.com, which is a paid, sponsored website that purports to "share information from so-called *adoption experts* about the unique connection linking adoption and health" according to the late Bill Pierce, the same Bill Pierce who headed National Committee For Adoption-NCFA lobby of Christian adoption agencies that has consistently *opposed* the 1980 Draft Model Adoption Act which addressed Adoptees' right to know their own pre-adoption medical information. The site also reveals, by clicking the "About" button, the following: "Adoption Medical News" brings you the most comprehensive group of *advertisers* in an easily navigated format" (*"advertisers"* including *drug companies*).

Called a "liar" and a "menace" by Green Ribbon Campaign adoption activists online, Dr. Laura Schlesinger told her audience that: *"Adoptees "don't need an updated family medical history when deciding to have children....No one needs a family medical history because all the tests are now available."* And Thomas C Atwood, who was serving as President and CEO of the National Council For Adoption (NCFA) and who previously served on the Board of Bethany Christian Services adoption agencies alleged as follows:

"Mandatory openness adds nothing to the adopted person's ability to obtain medical information. The increasing availability of genetic testing is making the issue of medical records moot. One can obtain information about one's genetic predisposition from such tests than from medical histories of biological parents. "
(Sources: *"Dr. Laura Show,"* CBS/Paramount Domestic Television. 10-19-00; and NCFA's *"Adoption Factbook,"* page 43)

In reality, genetic testing of Adoptees for "probabilities" with regard to **more than 4500 known genetically transmissable diseases** would not only be Draconian, it would also not even include all known illnesses and disorders, just the 35 most common ones, and is expensive -- ranging from hundreds of thousands of dollars. One would need to be clairvoyant to decide which ones to test. Equally important, one must understand that, by the time the Adoptee is exhibiting symptoms that may prompt testing for an undisclosed inheritable disease, it is too late to prevent it.

Also important is the difference between "statistical probabilities" and proof of familial occurrences with regard to specific illnesses and disorders.

ADOPTEES EXPERIENCES IN SCHOOL.

There had existed no studies *that asked Adoptees* to share their experiences within schools. Studies had presented the views of Adoptive Parents and teachers, psychologists, and social workers. While their perspectives are important to consider, Adoptive Parents and professionals cannot speak for the Adoptee. Only Adoptees can share their unique perspectives on personal experiences.

In 2012 - Elizabeth S, Donalds, PsyD, a Clinical Psychologist, conducted a survey. The study involved
  64 Adoptees over age 16 who had attended school;
  Ages were 18 to mid-60s;
  Most were adopted at birth to 1 year,
  70% were born in the United States
  and the others were from Columbia, England, Brazil, Mauritius, Canada, Russia, Lebanon, India and South Korea
  "First" language was: English, German, French, Russia, Armenian, Hind, Portuguese
  78% were female;
  21.7% were male;
  33% were age 32 to 41

Donalds asked Adoptees to respond to questions and share their experiences in school. The following research questions guided the study:
  1. Did the Adoptees experience problems in school related to their adoptions?
  2. What are Adoptees' perspectives on the competence of school professionals with whom they personally had contact regarding adoption?

One of the questions asked: As a child in school, who knew you were adopted?
  While a majority shared their adoption experiences with friends,
  52% of teachers, administrators, counselors and psychologists
    were unaware of the student's adoption; only 13.6% said they knew'
  67.2% reported that their adoption affected them academically in some way;
  32.8% reported their adoption did not impact, but as one student explained:

"It really didn't affect my school experience until it started affecting my entire life, school just kind of got looped into that. I started thinking about it more and more and I had feelings of being abandoned and not cared about, and suddenly school didn't matter anymore because nothing seemed to matter except finding answers. That's why my grades fell from As to Cs, or even Ds. I failed a few tests that I ordinarily would have passed."

And another shared her difficulty in school:

"I spent a lot of time being bombarded with thoughts and images regarding my adoption and having overwhelming emotions which I couldn't outwardly express. Later in school I found it increasingly difficult to concentrate and learn. My work started to go down hill. The teachers just said I was lazy and I got demoted to go to the lower class for most subjects. My parents just listened to what the teachers said. I didn't trust people with authority much after that, so those relationships suffered. I became more oppositional. There was no-one to talk to about my confused feelings, people didn't discuss emotions in those days, let alone adoption. You were just supposed to do as you were told and everything would be good. I did okay in the end, but it was only because I had an excellent home tutor for a year before I sat for my final exams."

Adoptees in the study expressed feelings of isolation and shame when unable to participate in "family tree" projects. Several described how the loss of their biological family and genetic connections impacted them in school: for example, not looking like one's siblings was brought up frequently and **"being raised culturally as a White person when skin color is Brown."**

One Adoptee in the study shared frustrating experiences with school professionals:

"It depended on the person, but most of the time, no one really got it. When I would try to explain why my feelings had been hurt, or why simple things had hurt my feelings, because of my issues of abandonment, most teachers and licensed therapists had no idea what I was feeling."

The research on the experience of Adoptees in school highlights the need for more sensitivity training for school professionals around adoption. (Source: Elizabeth S. Donalds, PsyD, *"Voices of Adoption: Stories and Experiences Within Schools,"* Antioch New England University, Keene, New Hampshire, 2012)

"ATTACHMENT THERAPY" DEATHS, 1985-2009

From 1989 to 2009, some "therapists," despite knowing that the child's loss of a nurturing biological parent is the un-fixable cause of their problems, and despite knowing of prior child deaths from the same "therapies," endeavored to "fix" Adoptees to prevent "broken adoptions" by employing "Attachment and Re-Birthing" techniques designed to emulate the birth experience. Whether this was done to placate Adoptive Parents who could afford it, or whether these professionals truly believed they could "fix" a child when the child's loss of a nurturing biological parent is the un-fixable cause, is unclear. What is known is that

at least 32 children died or were rescued
from "Attachment Therapies" and "Re-Birthings"

which are actually deadly assaults on children advanced by professionals as a "cure" for "Attachment Disorder,: commonly diagnosed when Adoptive Parents simply "didn't like" their adopted children, and, as a result, the adopted children "didn't like" their Adoptive Parents. In the "re-birthing" procedure, the child is wrapped in a blanket theoretically representing the birth canal, and forced to try to overcome the weight of one or more adults pressing against the child who is trying to make their way out of the blanket under their own power. In this crude and dangerous attempt to transform the "chosen child" into one "as born to" the Adoptive Parents in a *"forever family,"* the following adopted children have ended up abused, severely injured or *"forever dead"* (Their stories are detailed in *"Chosen Children 2019"* - available from Amazon.com and BN.co)

1989 - Jeanie Warren - at 19, she sued her therapist (Texas)
1990 - Andrea Swenson, 9 - committed suicide (Oklahoma)
1990s- Bobby Vernon Jr., 7, severely injured (Texas)
1994 - S.M. Abbott, 5 - Rescued (Minnesota)
1994 - Lucas Ciambrone, 7 - declared "Murdered" (Florida)

1995 - **Krystal Ann Tibbets**, 3 - Killed (Texas)
1996 - **David Alexander Polreis**, 2 - Killed (Russian Adoptee, Colorado)
1998 - **Roberta Evers**, 6 - Killed (Colorado)
2000 - **Candace Elizabeth Newmaker**, 10 - Killed (Colorado)
2000 - **Viktor Alexander Matthey (Viktor Sergievich Tulimov)**, 7 - Killed (Russian, Colorado)
2001 - **Logan Lynn Marr**, 5 - Killed (Maine)
2001 - **Dallas (last name withheld)**, 5 - Rescued (Colorado)
2002 - **"Hansen Adoptees"**, 4 & 5 - (Russian Adoptees, Colorado)
2002 - **Cassandra Kilpatrick**, 4 - Killed (Utah)
2003 - **Jessica Hagmann**, 2 - Killed (Russian, Virginia)
2003 - **Jackson Brothers (Bruce, 19; Keith; Tyrone, 10; Michael)** - Rescued (New Jersey)
2004 - **Christopher Forder**, 8 - Killed (Washington)
2005 - **Dennis Merryman, (Denis Uritsky)**, 8 - Killed (Maryland)
2005 - **Sasha Bignell, 11 - 7 and Unnamed Adopted Girl, 4** (Russian, Minnesota)
2005 - **Nina Hilt**, 2 - Killed (Russian, Virginia)
2005 - **Gravelle Siblings, 1 to 14** - Rescued (Ohio)
2005 - **Latham Adoptees, 5, 8, 9, 10** - Rescued (Hispanic, Georgia)
2005 - **Vasquez Children, 6, 9, 12, 13** - Rescued (California)
2006 - **Katia Seidel, adopted at age 8**, Rescued (Russian, Texas)
2006 - **Angie Arndt**, 7 - Killed (Wisconsin)
2007 - **Hepple Children, Girl 13, Boy 10** - Escaped, Rescued (New Mexico)
2007 - **Kathryn Amon, 9, adopted at age 2** - Rescued (Russian, North Carolina)
2008 - **Ashlee Bunch, 15 - adopted at age 4** - Committed Suicide (Washington)
2008 - **Rhoten Girl, 13**- Rescued (Panamanian, Missouri)
2009 - **Alexis "Lexie" Agyepong-Glover, 13**, developmentally disabled - Murdered (Virginia)
2009 - **Corbin Adoptees, 7, 8, 10, 12** - Rescued (Russian, Wisconsin)
2009 - **Nathaniel Craver, 7** - Killed (Russian, Pennsylvania)

While the "Nature versus Nurture" debate continues as to whether an Adoptee is the product of his genes or his environment, new insights on "behavioral epigenetics" may prove that traumatic experiences in our past, or even in our ancestor's past, leave "molecular scars" adhering to our DNA - for instance, in the case of Jews whose great-grandparents were chased from their Russian shetls; Chinese whose grandparents lived through the ravages of the Cultural Revolution; young immigrants from Africa whose parents survived massacres, and adults of every ethnicity who grew up with alcoholic or abusive parents -- but also "positive" ancestral experiences - may all carry within them more than just memories.

RE-HOMING

Re-homing is considered to be a new phenomenon whereby the adopted child is illegally relinquished directly via social media to another placement without attorneys, social workers or anyone else watching out for the safety and well-being of the child. A recent investigation by Reuters found Internet message boards dedicated to re-homing adopted children with a new child advertised *about once a week*. While legal adoptions are handled

through courts, a simple power-of-attorney document can shuffle kids to another caretaker. Reporters discovered that with such little oversight, children were sometimes abused in their second, or even third, re-homing.
(Sources: Tina Traster, *"Who Would Give Up an Adopted Child?"* New York Post, 10-12-11; *"Adoption Horror Story: Re-homing Adopted Children,"* Reuters Newswire, 9-16-13; and Emily Matcher, *"Broken Adoption: When Parents 'Rehome' Adopted Children."* TIME.com, 9-20-15.)

Some [adoptive] parents describe horrific behavioral and psychological problems on the part of children who have been abused or neglected before their adoptions [the article didn't specify whether the abuse occurred while in care of the "Birth" Parent(s) or not until trauma of family separation or a pre-adoption foster placement.] *'We have experienced multiple school expulsions, physical assaults, fires, psychiatric admissions, ER visits for self-mutilation, sexual acting out, stolen credit cards, multiple police calls, etc."* writes one Wisconsin father of an adopted son, commenting on a New York Times article:

"We don't have the slightest idea of what we're getting ourselves into and every school or social service agency basically told us we were on our own.'"
(Source: Emily Matcher, *"Broken Adoption: When Parents 'Rehome' Adopted Children,"* TIME.com, 9-20-15.)

ADOPTEE SUICIDES

In a study of suicide rates among adoptees versus children raised by biological parents, the mean age of the 1000 participants was about age 14; 56 had attempted suicide; 47 of those were adoptees. The odds of a reported suicide attempt were **4 times greater in adoptees** compared with non-adoptees (odds ratio: 4.23). (Source: Margaret A. Keyes, PhD, et al, *"Risk of Suicide in Adopted and Non-adopted Offspring,"* Journal of the American Academy of Pediatrics, Oct. 2013, 132(4) 639-646; http://www.ncbi.nlm.nih.gov/pmc/articles/PMC3784288/)

141 of 147 suicides involving drugs, from 1983 to 1993, were by Adoptees.
(Source: Brother Alex McDonald, Jesuit Priest, Youth Worker, Melbourne, Australia, 6-3-93)

In America, attempted suicide and actual suicide are more common among adolescent Adoptees than those who live with biological parents. A national longitudinal study was conducted of 7th and 12th grade students, in which Adoptees were found to differ significantly from non-Adoptees (Source: Gail Slap, MD; Elizabeth Goodman, MD; Ben Huang, MS-Pediatrics, in the Official Journal of Pediatrics, Vol. 108, No. 2, 8-1-01, p2)

In 2013, John Brooks wrote an article on his adopted daughter, Casey Brooks, and the issues inherent in intercountry adoption, after the teenager committed suicide by jumping off the Golden Gate Bridge in San Francisco. (Source: John Brooks, *"Adoption and Suicide: Casey's Story,"* Adoption Voice Magazine, 9-14-13)

ADOPTED BY LGBT ADOPTERS

58% of the children of lesbians called themselves "gay;"
33% of the children of gay men called themselves "gay" whereas only about
5% to 10% of the children of straight parents call themselves "gay." .
(Source: Study by Professor Walter Shumm, Kansas State University College
of Human Ecology Family Studies; and Paul Kix,
"Study: Gay Parents More Likely to Have Gay Kids," 10-17-10.)

The courts have struggled with the realities of the child's situation versus the desires of the adults in cases of gay, lesbian and transgender parenting, even enacting "Multiple Parents" Law (California) to fill gaps for Adopted children and Donor Offspring of LGBT parents. ACLU misspoke when referring to an LGBT "right" to adopt – No one has a "right" to adopt a stranger's child. Presently, one gay, lesbian, or transgender partner adopts the child of his/her partner, the child being conceived by Donor insemination in the case of two lesbian co-parents, or by a Surrogate in the case of two gay male co-parents. Whether the parents are gay or straight, and whether the child is Adopted or Donor conceived, or he is his parents' Biological child, ALL children struggle for **sexual identity and acceptance**, and so it seems unfair to add burdens of his parents' struggles with infertility, sexual identity and acceptance.

RAPE AND INCEST

RAPE:

22% of Adoptees fear they will find they are the product of Rape
Adoptees are also vulnerable to being raped:
The highest incidence of Rape was reported in IL, AZ, CA
1 out 10 victims were Male;
40% of perpetrators were Male Adopters;

20% of perpetrators were Male Adoptive Siblings

(Source: 100 National Collective Surveys of Adult Adoptees born 1933-1973.
National Center for Victims of Crime)

Child molesters are usually a close family member, or family friend;
A majority of child *victims* of sexual predators are Adoptees."
(Source: FBI statistics)

**46% of all children who are raped are victims of family members;
11% are raped by fathers or step-fathers.**
(Source: National Center for Victims of Crime)

**30% of children molested "in the family" are a stepchild, *adopted.*
or foster child; only 19% are the biological child.**
(Source: U.S. Census Statistical Abstract, 1999)

**Only 10% of child sexual abusers
report that they molest a child who is a stranger.**
(Source: Abel and Harlow Child Molestation Research and Prevention Study).

Abusers who have adopted children may rationalize that because the Adoptee is not the biological child of the Adoptees. the child is "fair game.")

**27% of adult female sex offenders, but only
16% of male sex offenders *admitted* to having been sexually abused in childhood.**
(Source: psychiatrists Perry and Szalavitz, in *"The Boy Who Was Raised As A Dog,"* 2006)

90% of efforts go to protect children from abusers who are strangers

when what is needed is to focus 90% of efforts toward protecting children from molesters in their own families and who are friends of their families. (Source: Policy statement by Child Molestation Research and Prevention Institute Inc. Oakland, California, 2009).

Many adult female and male Adoptees have, over the past several decades, gone public with their stories of sexual abuse (i.e. child rape) by their male Adopters. Many shared such stories with this writer as well (in *"Chosen Children"* on Amazon). Unfortunately, Adoptees' claims of sexual abuse are most often ignored or disbelieved, unless a celebrity is involved, but even then, "coverup" is pervasive. One well-known example was Dylan Farrow, the adopted daughter of actor-screen writer, Woody Allen and his then-girlfriend, Mia Farrow. In 2014, for the first time, she spoke out, accusing Allen of sexually abusing her in 1993 when she was 7 years old. At that time, headlines revealed allegations of Allen abusing Dylan, along with the sexual relationship with Farrow's Mia Farrow's and Allen's older, consenting, adopted daughter, Sun Yi, and the split between Allen and Farrow. But after a custody hearing that denied Allen further visitation rights, Farrow declined to press criminal charges against Allen due to (in the Prosecutor's words) "the fragility of the child victim, Dylan." (Source: Dylan Farrow, with Note by Nicholas Krstof, in *"An Open Letter From Dylan Farrow,"* New York Times, 2-1-14)

Another example of an adopted child victim speaking out in adulthood is that of Matt Sandusky, adopted son of ex-Penn State Coach, Jerry Sandusky, convicted serial child rapist. Jerry Sandusky hasn't been charged with abusing his adopted son; the ex-coach cannot be charged criminally, based on his son's accusations, due to the statute of limitations. Matt's "Birth" Mother, Debra Long, fought the court system over her son's placement in the home of the former Penn State assistant football coach, who was convicted of sexually abusing 10 boys -- and in a December 2011 interview with the *AP*, Long said that Sandusky was pushy, controlling and had estranged Matt from his "birth" family, but that Centre County's court system ignored her concerns because of Sandusky's stature. (Source: *"Jerry Sandusky Case: Matt Sandusky's Biological Mom Raised Concerns About the Former PSU Coach As Far Back As 1994,"* CBS News/AP - 6-27-12)

Profilers now know that most Sex Offenders have, themselves, been sexually abused childhood So it is not surprising that Adoptees who are at risk of being sexually abused by their Adopters are also at risk of becoming Sex Offenders.

New Zealand found that **adult Adoptees can better cope with such traumatic revelations as discovering they are a child of Rape, than with not having any information.** Many had already fantasized the event and can handle it. Most Adoptees know that in exploring the unknown void of their origins, anything is possible, realizing that there must have been difficulties or they would not have been placed for adoption. This information remaining secret increases the shame. The reality, once it is confronted, is less than the enormity of the secret.

One Adoptee conceived from rape said, "When we met things were pretty tense between us. I knew that my "Birth" Mother was holding back something. I asked her and she told me. We both held each other and shared exactly what had happened and we shared our hurts and fears. It was one of my "Birth" Mother's fears that one day I would find her and ask her. And now that the traumatic time passed, somehow in the sharing of our deep personal grief feelings, we built up a relationship. We now understand each other on an issue that no one seems to understand." (Source: Keith C. Griffith, *"The Right to Know Who You Are,"* Katherine Kimbell, pub. 1992)

INCEST:

Adolescent and adult Adoptees as well as social workers, have expressed concern about **"unintended incest"** due to sealed records preventing Adoptees from knowing with whom they are biologically related. Consensual sex between adults (18 years or older), even between close family members, is **lawful** in the Netherlands and Belgium, but in Florida, for instance, consensual sex with someone known to be your aunt, uncle, niece or nephew constitutes a **Third Degree Felony.** Medical risks to a child born of First Degree Relationships (parent, child, siblings who share half of each other's genes) are:

31.4% or death and severe defect
6.8% to 11.2% for significant birth defects
(extrapolated from First Cousin data)

Half-siblings share 1/4 of each other's genes, which does not mean the risk is reduced by half, only that there is still a significant risk of severe birth defects resulting from such unions.

In Germany, a case of incest publicized internationally, concerned consenting adult Adoptees, Patrick Stubing and Susan Karolewski, who *knew* that they were biological brother and sister, before they had 4 children together. They were prosecuted and served jail time. According to court records, the first 3 of their children have mental and physical disabilities and were placed in foster care. In April, 2012, Patrick Stubing lost his case that the conviction violated his right to a private family life. (Source: Der Spiegel, a German news source, 2012)

In Georgia, adult adopted siblings, Joel Lee Domingues and Melissa Fuss Able, unaware of their biological sibling relationship, had a daughter together. Joel claimed he was already intimately involved with Melissa *before* he learned of their biological relationship while Melissa's biological mother, Sandra Cano Sauceda, claimed that Melissa *knew* but intentionally withheld this from Joel. (Source: *"Blood Relatives: A True Story of Family Secrets and Murders,"* Access Press 2013)

ADOPTEES DENIED ACCESS TO MEDICAL INFORMATION 1981-2014

1981 - *Newsweek* (10/81) reported the plight of James Grant George, an adult Adoptee, when Kansas City, Missouri, Judge Gene Martin said "No" to his request to open his court file in order to discover his parents' identities. George had leukemia and needed a bone marrow transplant from a blood relative to save his life. The judge ruled *"Although the circumstances were dire, they were not compelling enough to open his adoption file."* George's comment to media: *"If I were a convicted murderer, the governor could give me a pardon. Obviously, the 'crime of illegitimacy' is not pardonable in the state of Missouri."*

1986 - This writer asked Judge Glenn E. Knierim, Connecticut's probate court administrator, to give my son's Adoptive Parents my updated medical information and my physician's letter regarding my *inheritable* cardiac disorder and inheritable allergies to at least 10 cardiac medications. Knierim responded *"under state law, I have no authority to take such action."* (Source: Chris Janis *"Mom Hunts for Son She Gave Up,"* The New Haven Register, Connecticut, 4-12-87)

1988 - Nancy L. Fisher, MD, MPH, Society of Human Genetics, Seattle, Washington, and AmFOR, began polling the states and determined that Adoptees' background information, including medical, was not routinely collected.

1989 - When Brian Wilkins informed his Adoptive Parents he had AIDS and wanted to locate his mother before it was too late, his male Adoptive Parents then declared he "had no son." That's when Brian Wilkins decided to become Hawk Ramsay. "Ramsay" is the name of his mother who gave him up for adoption when he was an infant and "Hawk" reflects his Cherokee and Choctaw roots as well as the nickname he earned while serving on the U. S. S. Kitty Hawk. "Hawk" found his mother who was supportive of her son until the end.
(Source: The Desert Sun, Palm Springs, California, 5-4-89):

1990 - AmFOR's "open records" lobbying and its televised Adoptee-Parent reunions drew public awareness about adoption issues, as did *Carangelo, Schafrick v. O'Neill, State of CT, The Children's Center, et al,* especially about the problem of Adoptees' lack of true and current family medical information. By 1990, mandatory collection of such information at the time of relinquishment, as well as mandatory disclosure of "non-identifying background information," had become law in most states. *Carangelo v. O'Neill (Weicker)* reached the U.S. Supreme Court certiori denied *("Carangelo v. Connecticut"* on Amazon)

1996 - At age 21, Brian Bauman, born Kim Sung Duk in South Korea in 1974, who had been adopted at age 3 by Steve and Elaine Bauman of Minnesota, was diagnosed with chronic Myelogenous Leukemia. He was told he would die within 5 years if he didn't receive a bone-marrow transplant. Brian's story was publicized in 1995 in Korea's major media. The newspaper, *Hankook Ilbo,* was flooded with letters from Korean parents who had surrendered children in the past. *The Korean Broadcasting System* conducted its own search with help from the eastern Child Welfare Society which had placed Brian. Mother and son were secretly reunited but neither she nor his 33-year old sibling were a tissue match for bone marrow transplantation, but an unrelated Korean donor was found as result of the publicity, and over the next few months thousands of Koreans volunteered to place their names on two donor transplant registries (Source: "Korea Saves a Son," TIME International, 7-15-96)

1996 - Terminal Illness Emergency Search (TIES) website describes their first case (12-96): An Adoptee with AIDS named Grady wanted to find his mother before it was too late but the court and agency that held his mother's identity would not oblige. Deb Schwartz, then TIES Coordinator, rallied volunteers via Internet and in less than 24 hours, Grady was reunited with his mother by phone.

1998 - Adoptee, Michelle Robertson shared her life and-death struggle to get the Monroe County, New York court to open her adoption file in order to discover her parents' identities. Roberts had Hodgkin's Disease and required a bone marrow transplant from a biological relative to save her life. The court denied her request. (Source: NBC TV Extra, 8-14-98)

1998 - Barbara Casali-Mingus, 31, was a 1967 *"gray market"* Adoptee ("gray market" meaning money was paid "under the table" but correct paperwork legalized the adoption). She found her biological mother. The reunion was amicable but saddened by the fact that her mother was dying of cancer. Her mother admonished her to "be checked for the disease." Mingus said "I told her I had been checked last year. She said that didn't matter, *to get checked again anyway. I did and discovered I have cervical cancer.* I had an operation and recovered. She saved my life." (Source: The Albany Democrat-Herald /AP, 7-30-98)

1998 - Shreveport Juvenile Court Judge Gallagher said "No" to Leonard Hargrove Jobron, a 50-year old Adoptee whose daughter had leukemia. Leonard's illnesses precluded him from being a suitable donor for his daughter and the Donor Bank had found no match in 2 years.
(Source: The Shreveport Times, Louisiana, 9-8-98)

1999   - Anna Bound was an Adoptee, wife and mother. Her baby was sick. His condition could not be diagnosed. Doctors needed Anna's medical history to treat him. The adoption agency wanted $800 for the information which she could not afford. A few months later, Anna died unexpectedly from an *inherited* disorder she didn't know she had. She left behind a grieving husband and child. Anna was 24 years old. (Source: *"Dying To Know You,"* Delaware Reunion Registry website, 7-17-99)

1999 - Adoptee Curtis Endicott died of a lifelong undiagnosed lung ailment on 9-11-99 at age 51 while waiting for Oregon's successful Adoptee Rights Initiative (Measure 58) to take effect. Measure 58 (HB 3194) passed by a strong margin in the November 1998 election but was held up by a court injunction. Endicott had been an active campaigner in support of the measure and an active participant in the ensuing lawsuit in which he had been granted intervener status. (Source: Dan Wrather, news anchor, CBS Evening News, 9-13-99)

2000 - Adoptee Deborah Baker O'Connor, born at Willows Maternity Home 4-17-47, lost her battle with leukemia, never having found her family. (Source: Post on website (1-25-00) for former Willows Maternity Home mothers and Adoptees at http://member.tripod.com/~bedgie/thewillows.html)

2000 - An Internet website for searching Adoptees and parents posted this message: "William Ferguson, born 'Baby Boy Stephens' in Modesto, CA., 2-8-52, to Janet Stephens from Ceres, CA. is searching for a Live Liver Donor. He has already lost his son to leukemia in 1997 at age 10 for lack of a matching donor." (Source: Adoptee Birthfamily Connection, 6-24-00)

2000 - Adoptee Susan Martin was diagnosed with leukemia. Martin, 34, requested any documents to which she is entitled from Boston's Department of Social Services. She hoped to use them to locate her blood relatives and made a second potentially life-altering decision—to also search for her own biological son given up for adoption almost 18 years prior. All these agencies would do is place Martin's information in a file until the other party should inquire. *(Source: "Second Chances: Adoption's Secret Terminally Ill. Woman Seeking Biological Past,"* The Boston Globe, 12-11-00)

2001 - The Korean Organ Donor Program campaigned to help a Korean Adoptee living in the U.S. and suffering from leukemia. (Source: *"Citizens Campaign for Bone Marrow Donation for Adoptee, Korean-American,"* The Korean Herald, 5-23-01)

2001 – A website for searching Adoptees and Parents posted: "Emergency Search: male Adoptee, born 5-27-53, Kansas City, has leukemia." (Source: D's Search Posts website, 6-2-01).

2001 - Melinda Kerner, a 40-year old Adoptee and mother of 2 children, ages 5 and 9 had leukemia and her doctor gave her about 5 years to live. Kerner paid the adoption agency the non-refundable fee they require to do a

"search" for her parents, then reported that her parents "declined to release their names to Kerner." Kerner was then in remission thanks to a new experimental drug but her prognosis could not be predicted. A bone marrow transplant would have been better. (Source: Diane Costanzo, in *"I Am A Medical Miracle,"* Ladies Home Journal, p. 76, 12-01)

2001 - Tami Brundage, 27-year old Holt International Adoptee from Korea, was diagnosed with leukemia. Holt's file says she was "abandoned." When Tami was taken in by Holt, it was the practice of Holt-Korea to falsify birth names and declare their wards as "abandoned" *even when the mother's names were known.* The children's health information and ages were often falsified as well, to make them more appealing to potential Adoptive Parents in the U.S., so they have no "paper trail." (Source: Holt International's page at holtintl.org/brundage.shtml, 12-15-01).

2002 - Elaine Tomasini, an Adoptee born 2-3-62 in Buffalo, New York on 5-20-01, asked AmFOR for search assistance to locate her biological family. Tomasini had leukemia. A bone marrow transplant from a relative could save her life, but their identities were sealed in her adoption file. (Source: AmFOR's "The Open Record" newsletter archives)

2014 - Laws and policies still vary from state to state as to how much medical information is collected, and how it is maintained and disclosed. It is usually summarized by a case worker, not updated and usually not accessible on demand to those it most concerns. (Source: Mary Carol Randall, MA, *"Adoptees Genetic Information,"* Genetic Health website)

2018 – Statisical compilations such as *"The Adoption and Donor Conception Factbook,"* adoption-themed documentaries such as *"Chosen Children 2019,"* and "true crime" books such as *"RAGE – How An Adoption Ignites a Fire,"* and the soon to be released *"No Remorse – 400 Adopted Killers"* further support the above facts by putting a name and a face to the special interests and victims.

INDEX

ABOUT THE AUTHOR

LORI CARANGELO is no stranger to the criminal world – as a long-time interviewer, correspondent, and confident to incarcerated killers, rapists, gang members, and assorted other criminals. She compiles their stories, not solely to satisfy the reader's thirst for a bloody murder tale, but to ferret out clues to often asked questions such as *WHY* they did it, *HOW* a normal child grew to become a "monster," and *WHERE* the bodies are hidden.

Born in 1945 to Italian-American parents in New Haven, Connecticut, she is retired from 25 years of government and private sector administrative positions in Santa Barbara and Palm Desert, California.

Lori has authored more than 25 non-fiction paperback and e-books currently on Amazon -- from cookbooks to adoption-themed documentaries, to true crime stories.

Also by Lori Carangelo:
and available on Amazon:

ADOPTED KILLERS
430 Adoptees Who Killed – How and Why They Did It
SERIAL KILLERS ON THE INTERSTATE -
200 Highway Killers by State
KONDRO
The "Uncle Joe" Killer
JAMES MUNRO
And the Freeway Killers
ESPOSITO
The First Mafioso
EYEWITNESS
The Case of the Carefully Crafted Central Coast Rapist
THE 8 BALL CAFÉ
Stories of Adoption, Addiction and Redemption
BLOOD RELATIVES
A True Story of Family Secrets and Murders
CHOSEN CHILDREN 2019
Poeple as Commodities in America's Failed
Foster Care, Adoption and Immigration Systems
CARANGELO v. CONNECTICUT
A Case of Lifelong Opposition to
Government Protected Child Stealing
THE ULTIMATE SEARCH BOOK
U.S. and Worldwide Editions
THE ADOPTION AND DONOR CONCEPTION FACTBOOK
The Only Comprehensive Source of U.S. & Global Data
on the Hidden Families of Foster Care, Adoption and Donor Conception

www.ingramcontent.com/pod-product-compliance
Lightning Source LLC
Chambersburg PA
CBHW071452070426
42452CB00039B/1141